WHERE DO NUDISTS KEEP THEIR HANKIES?

Also by Mitchell Symons

NON-FICTION

Forfeit!

The Equation Book of Sports Crosswords

The Equation Book of Movie Crosswords

The You Magazine Book of Journalists (four books, co-author)

Movielists (co-author)

The Sunday Magazine Book of Crosswords

The Hello! Magazine Book of Crosswords (three books)

How To Be Fat: The Chip And Fry Diet (co-author)

The Book of Criminal Records

The Book of Lists

The Celebrity Lists Book

The Celebrity Sex Lists Book

The Bill Clinton Joke Book

National Lottery Big Draw 2000 (co-author)

That Book

This Book

The Other Book

The Sudoku Institute Puzzle Book (co-author)

Why Girls Can't Throw

FICTION

All In

The Lot

WHERE DO NUDISTS KEEP THEIR HANKIES?

...and other ^ADULT questions you always wanted answered

Mitchell Symons

BANTAM PRESS

LONDON · TORONTO · SYDNEY · AUCKLAND · JOHANNESBURG

TRANSWORLD PUBLISHERS
61–63 Uxbridge Road, London W5 5SA, a division of The Random House Group Ltd

RANDOM HOUSE AUSTRALIA (PTY) LTD
20 Alfred Street, Milsons Point, Sydney, New South Wales 2061, Australia

RANDOM HOUSE NEW ZEALAND LTD
18 Poland Road, Glenfield, Auckland 10, New Zealand

RANDOM HOUSE SOUTH AFRICA (PTY) LTD
Isle of Houghton, Corner of Boundary Road & Carse O'Gowrie,
Houghton 2198, South Africa

Published 2006 by Bantam Press, a division of Transworld Publishers

A catalogue record for this book is available from the British Library.

ISBN 978 0593 05644 8 (from Jan 07)
ISBN 0593 05644 2

Designed by www.carrstudio.co.uk
Printed by Mackays of Chatham Ltd, Chatham, Kent

1 3 5 7 9 10 8 6 4 2

Papers used by Transworld Publishers are natural, recyclable products
made from wood grown in sustainable forests. The manufacturing processes conform to the
environmental regulations of the country of origin.

To Penny and Jack with all my love

INTRODUCTION

'Is sex dirty?' asked Woody Allen before answering his own question with the line: 'Only if you're doing it right.' Let me pose a rhetorical question of my own: is sex funny? Indeed, is there a more hilarious sight than a man before, during or after the act of sex?

And part of what makes sex so comical is the fact that people are so damn serious about it.

As a happily married man, I'm more than content to watch from the sidelines – so to speak – making snide and unhelpful comments at all the ridiculous participants.

Anything for a chuckle.

Of course, I've got form in this area. Although my last book (*Why Girls Can't Throw*) wasn't specifically about sex, I managed to sneak in lots of sexual questions – such as:

- **If you were supple enough to give yourself a blow job, would that make you gay?**

- **Why are lesbians called dykes?**

- **Why is the name 'John Thomas' used as a nickname for the penis?**

- **All right, are those rumours about Richard Gere and gerbils true?**

- Is it true that Catherine the Great died having sex with her horse?

- Is it true that Marianne Faithfull once had a foursome with Mick Jagger, Keith Richards and a Mars Bar?

- Do women who live/work together menstruate at the same time?

- What is the origin of the use of the word 'gay' to mean homosexual?

- Who was the best-endowed celebrity of all time?

- Has anyone ever died during sex?

- Do women have wet dreams too?

- Who was the first woman to 'lie back and think of England'?

Well, now I've decided to devote a whole book to questions about sex.

Of course, I'm just a middle-aged man who's convinced that everyone's having more fun than me. One of the more unfortunate aspects of the human condition is the fear that you're missing out. It was ever thus. As Michael Caine said of the 1960s, 'Swinging London was the same two hundred people in the King's Road sleeping with each other.' I was never one of the two hundred – except maybe for a two-month period in 1981 when every girl seemed to say yes and … well, I don't expect you to accompany me on that particular trip down memory lane.

In any event, other people's sex lives are more interesting than your own. Even if, in truth, they're not.

Clearly, I'm no sex expert but then who is? I suppose 'sex experts' are but they do take sex so bloody seriously. I had a run-in with these people once which illustrates this perfectly. It happened about 20 years ago. I used to write regular features for *Penthouse*. They were a bit 'naughty' but also really funny – in many ways the best things I ever wrote. Alas, all my contributions will have been lost: I shouldn't think any copies have survived the purges that soon-to-be-attached young men are obliged to go through – hence the piles of ripped-up jazz mags you find on rubbish tips.

Anyway, I got a call from the then editor of *Forum*, the bible for the sexually serious, asking me to go through all the small ads from the past year and, from them, put together a sexual map of Britain.

A job's a job and, as a freelance (then as now), my only question was how much?

So I started scanning the small ads and I was soon astonished by how much I didn't know. There were perversions – 'preferences' as the editor corrected me – that were just unbelievable. One was infibulation, which, I gathered through a fug of terror, involved your loved one putting a tiny padlock through your genital area. Well, not my loved one – at least not while I had any strength in my body.

Anyway, I wrote the piece as well as I could – I'm a dab hand with stats thanks to a lifetime addiction to *Wisden* – but I couldn't resist spiking it with gags. I recall writing about infibulation that while I respected the diversity of other people's sex lives, I had to report a nightmare I'd had in which I was late with my copy and the editor came round with a giant padlock …

It didn't go down well. Nor, in fact, did any of my *bons mots*. When I protested to the editor that sex was funny and should be treated as such, she explained to me that *Forum* readers took it seriously – very seriously. They were used to sexologists who also took sex seriously – very seriously.

I never wrote for the magazine again and have had contempt for sexologists – amateur and professional – ever since.

However, that's not to say that I'm without back-up in this area.

My friends and acquaintances include: several gays and lesbians, two men who became women, one woman who became a man, several adulterers, a satyr, a former prostitute, a celibate and a couple who have an 'open marriage'. I also have two teenage sons – although I've promised them I'll only consult them in an emergency. I also have access to doctors, zoologists, philosophers and psychiatrists.

In case you think that I'm kind of louche or anything, I should say that I doubt that my friends and acquaintances are any more outré or sophisticated than yours: my guess is that your circle contains a remarkably similar mix, it's just that you've never delved that deep.

Fortunately, as my friends have often had cause to remark, I lack both the tact and the embarrassment genes and so am totally uninhibited about asking incredibly personal questions. I'm driven by two specific things: a very low threshold of boredom on the one hand and almost insatiable curiosity on the other. It's a toxic mix that sometimes makes my wife wince with embarrassment (she, alas for her, has the e. gene) and occasionally loses us friends but, at long last, I can put it to some practical use.

So here are a hundred or so questions of a sexual orientation: breezy not sleazy; entertaining not titillating – if any bloke reading this gets a hard-on then I will have failed. (If, on the other hand, any woman – any extremely cute woman – finds herself getting incredibly aroused by something I've written, then my email address can be found at the back of the book. I am, of course, happily married and totally monogamous but, hey, everything's negotiable ...)

Mitchell Symons

You like to do *what*?
(Or how perverted is perverted?)

*'The only unnatural sex act is that
which you cannot perform'*

Alfred Kinsey

In some ways this is the signature question for the whole book in the sense that it covers the waterfront. My first port of call was good old Google. I put in 'sexual practices' but after tiptoeing smartly around the sort of sites you really don't want your wife to find in your browser, I went offline and consulted the books in my really rather impressive library (where size counts) – especially *The Encyclopaedia of Unusual Sexual Practices* – and found a range of activities from the hey-that's-me-I-didn't-know-it-had-a-name! to the sounds-fun to the not-for-me-but-I-can-get-my-head-around-it to the why-would-anyone-want-to-do-that/how-did-anyone-even-think-of-that to the oh-my-god-just-don't-go-there.

So you get an idea, let me give you examples from each category (omitting any 'preferences' that will be the subject of separate questions).

HEY-THAT'S-ME-I-DIDN'T-KNOW-IT-HAD-A-NAME!
Allorgasmia: fantasizing about someone other than one's partner
Basoexia: being aroused by kissing
Gymnophilia: being aroused by nudity
Mammagymnophilia: being aroused by breasts

SOUNDS-FUN

Antholagnia: being aroused by smelling flowers

Axillism: rubbing of penis in an armpit

Bigynist: sex between one male and two females (it only!)

Coitus à mammilla: rubbing of penis between breasts

Coitus à unda: sex or sex games in water

Tripsophilia: being aroused by massage

NOT-FOR-ME-BUT-I-CAN-GET-MY-HEAD-AROUND-IT

Acousticophilia: being aroused by sounds

Acrophilia: being aroused by heights or high altitudes

Agonophilia: being aroused by partner pretending to struggle

Agrexophilia: being aroused by others knowing you are having sex

Albutophilia: being aroused by water

Amaurophilia: preference for a blind or blindfolded sex partner

Anasteemaphilia: attraction to taller or shorter partners

Androminetophilia: being aroused by female partner who dresses like male

Amomaxia: sex in parked car

Autopederasty: person inserting their own penis into their anus

Capnolagnia: being aroused by watching others smoke

'The only unnatural sexual behaviour is none at all' Sigmund Freud

Dacryphilia: person who is aroused by seeing their partner cry

Dendrophilia: being aroused by tree or fertility worship of them

Dogging: couples who engage in sex in their car while others watch from outside

Doraphilia: being aroused by animal fur, leather, or skin

Erotographomania: being aroused by writing love poems or letters

Frottage: rubbing body against partner or object for arousal

Genuphallation: insertion of penis between the knees of a partner

Gynemimetophilia: being aroused by a male impersonating a female

Hirsutophilia: being aroused by armpit hair

Hodophilia: being aroused by travelling

Knismolagnia: being aroused by tickling

Lactaphilia: being aroused by lactating breasts

Lygerastia: tendency to be aroused only in darkness

Maieusiophilia: being aroused by pregnant women

Melolagnia: being aroused by music

Moriaphilia: being aroused by telling sexual jokes

Nasophilia: being aroused by noses

Neophilia: being aroused by novelty or change

Oculophilia: being aroused by eyes

Odontophilia: being aroused by teeth

Olfactophilia: being aroused by smells

Podophilia: being aroused by feet

Pygophilia: being aroused by contact with buttocks

Trichophilia: being aroused by hair

Xenophilia: being aroused by strangers

Zelophilia: being aroused by jealousy

WHY-WOULD-ANYONE-WANT-TO-DO-THAT/HOW-DID-ANYONE-EVEN-THINK-OF-THAT

Acrotomophilia: sexual preference for amputees

Agalmatophilia: being aroused by statues

Algophilia: being aroused by experiencing pain

Androidism: being aroused by robots with human features

Apotemnophilia: person who has sexual fantasies about losing a limb

Arachnephilia: being aroused by spiders

Asphyxiaphilia: being aroused by lack of oxygen

Asthenolagnia: being aroused by weakness or being humiliated

Autassassinophilia: being aroused by orchestrating one's own death by the hands of another

Ball dancing: self-flagellation by hanging fruit from hooks in skin

Blood sports: sex games that involve blood

Belonephilia: being aroused by use of needles

Catheterophilia: being aroused by use of catheters

Chezolagnia: masturbating while defecating

Coprophilia: being aroused by playing with faeces

Entomophilia: being aroused by insects

Eproctophilia: being aroused by flatulence

Formicophilia: sex play with ants

Harmatophilia: being aroused by sexual incompetence or mistakes, usually in female partner

Harpaxophilia: being aroused by being robbed or burgled

Hemotigolagnia: being aroused by bloody sanitary pads

Hierophilia: being aroused by sacred objects

Homilophilia: being aroused by hearing or giving sermons

Iantronudia: being aroused by exposing oneself to a doctor

Idrophrodisia: being aroused by BO, especially from the genitals

Kleptophilia: being aroused by stealing

Klismaphilia: being aroused by enemas

Menophilia: being aroused by menstruating women

Mysophilia: being aroused by dirt

Ophidiophilia: being aroused by snakes

Pecattiphilia: being aroused by sinning or possibly guilt

Pediophilia: being aroused by dolls

Peodeiktophilia: exhibitionism

Phobophilia: being aroused by fear or hate

Phygephilia: being aroused by being a fugitive

Psychrophilia: arousal from being cold or watching others freeze

Pyrophilia: being aroused by fire or its use in sex play

Scopophilia: being aroused by getting stared at

Siderodromophilia: being aroused by trains

Taphephilia: being aroused by getting buried alive

OH-MY-GOD-JUST-DON'T-GO-THERE

Autophagy: self-cannibalism or eating one's own flesh

Autosadism: infliction of pain or injury on oneself

Brachioprotic eroticism: a deep form of fisting where the arm enters the anus

Dysmorphophilia: being aroused by physical impairment

Emetophilia: being aroused by vomit

Nosophilia: being aroused by knowing partner has terminal illness

Symphorophilia: being aroused by arranging a disaster or explosion

Anything involving children, incest, violence and degradation. Oh yes, and necrophilia – sex with corpses.

OK, so that's how I rate those different 'preferences' but my reactions are necessarily idiosyncratic. What I consider fun or reasonable might shock you and (almost certainly) vice versa. I guess the bottom line is that whatever consenting adults consent to do in private is entirely their business. But note the importance of the three operative words: consenting (and that consent must carry with it the ability to consent), adults and private.

* * * *

After putting together the above list, I emailed it to my friend Rick, whom I've already trailed as a satyr (dictionary definition: 'a man with strong sexual desires' – yup, that's Rick). He phoned me and said, 'You prig!' (I might have misheard him.) 'Just because you're a boring little fart who has sex three times a week and then only in the missionary position, how DARE you judge what other people get up to? For your information, you prick' – I heard him right that time – 'I have done several of the things that you say 'aren't for you', a few of the things that you're too fucking timid to have even considered – or so you say – and, yes, there are one or two things on your oh-my-god-just-don't-go-there-because-I'm-such-a-fucking-prude list that I'd be prepared to consider because, unlike you, I'm open-minded!'

Such as?

'Go fuck yourself!'

I was about to say, 'I would but I'm not an autopederast' (see above), but he'd hung up, leaving me yelping, 'I'm not a prude!' – the four words which, as I reflected later, do more than any others to mark out … yes, the prude.

What do men *really* want?

I canvassed all my male friends and acquaintances on this one and, perhaps unsurprisingly, the consensus was as follows:

1. To get it and …

2. … to get away with it.

What do women *really* want?

That's me in the spotlight, resisting the temptation to say, 'Who cares?' As a man, I start from the assumption that men want sex whereas women want ... well, so much more.

Now I know I'm generalizing – no, *really*? – but there's something in this, you know, and it's more, much more than the fact that women need foreplay and affection and bloody telephone calls afterwards, whereas men just want a quick shag.

There is, I suspect, a different biological imperative at work here.

To confirm my suspicion, I went to visit my tame social anthropologist, Dr Lorraine Mackintosh, which was no hardship as she is, as I have remarked in another book, no pig to look at.

Is there, I asked, a biological imperative at work here?

'That's the trouble with you hacks: you get hold of an expression – like biological imperative – and you start tossing it around like a, like a ...'

Salad?

'You know what I mean. In fact, you're not entirely wrong. There *is* a biological imperative at work here. Irrespective of the fact that 21st-century women act differently from their cavewomen ancestors, a surprising number of atavistic fears and drives persist. Chief among these is to procure the seed of the alpha male and then to find a male – not necessarily the same one – to help nurture that offspring. The man, on the other hand, just wants to spread his seed as far and as wide as possible.'

So a bloke wants to screw around whereas a bird wants the full works?

'Er, not quite.'

OK, can we say that, for men, having sex is the end – the aim, if you like – but that for women, it's just the beginning?

'No, not really. Yes, biologically, men want to impregnate as many women as possible, but women don't necessarily want to hang on to their men forever. This is also an explanation of why some women – many of us, if we're honest – are attracted to bastards. Do you remember how I said that women didn't necessarily need the same man to impregnate them and then provide for the child?'

Yes.

'Well, that's terribly important to bear in mind. The woman needs the very best seed and that's likely to belong to the alpha male who is, in turn, likely to be a bit of a bastard. Having got herself impregnated by this man, she now has her work cut out to keep him because *his* instinct is to go off and spread his seed. The trouble is that the very qualities she was searching for in a biological father for her child are unlikely to coincide with the qualities she'll need from the man who will support her and this child. Hence the conflict between the bastard and the nice guy.'

So how is this conflict resolved?

'Doesn't he look like his father?'

'Good question. Very often it's not. The girl finds her bastard but, before long, he's off screwing around. Alternatively, she has her good old Mr Dependable who's always there for her but she finds him dull and boring and so she starts to stray …'

What, in search of a bastard?

'Precisely,' said Dr M, rewarding me with a dazzling smile.

So we're doomed then, are we, as a species?

'No. Obviously not! The alpha male can learn to suppress his wandering and apply his superiority over his fellow males to the task of making lots of money for his family. After all, it's in the alpha male's interests to produce successful offspring—'

And sticking around to raise them is probably a better bet than screwing around – or, as we experts call it, the scattergun approach.

'There's a fascinating thing you should know about the male. What's the first thing his mother-in-law says after his wife – her daughter – has given birth? "Doesn't he look like his father?" That's right, the mother-in-law's role is to help solidify the father's bond to his child and the best way to do that is to persuade him that it is indeed his child.'

Fascinating.

'As for the sturdy dependable type – the antithesis, if you like, to the alpha male – his relationship with his wife can thrive if she can project on to him the sort of alpha-male qualities she yearns for.'

Which explains why the most unlikely blokes are touted as tigers by their wives. But does this help to explain what women want?

She giggled. 'No, but it does go some way to explaining the dynamics behind mate-selection. As for what women want from a man, this woman wants chocolate and lots of it.'

Is it different for men?

If the 'it' is cheating – which of course it is – then I refer you to the earlier answer. Yes, it is. It might even be necessary for the survival of the species.

There are biological imperatives and atavistic urges that do make it different for men, but does that justify such behaviour?

My own view is that it doesn't. We may be programmed to behave in a certain way but that doesn't mean we shouldn't do our best to rise above it. I have a friend – more of an acquaintance really – who (at the last count) was boasting of three ongoing dalliances.

Even though I haven't identified him (though he'll know who he is), it might be fair to contrast him with another friend/acquaintance who *doesn't* cheat on his wife but loses no opportunity to run her down to anyone prepared to listen (aye, and many who aren't).

So which is better – even if we can begin to define what we mean by the word 'better'? The unfaithful husband who is loyal to his wife or the faithful husband who is disloyal about his wife? I certainly prefer the former – if only because I can't bear the latter's whingeing – but, ultimately, they're just as bad as each other: that much infidelity amounts to disloyalty (it isn't so much the sex as the pillow talk and, worse still, the inevitable deceit), while that much disloyalty can only be corrosive to the marriage.

Perhaps we should devise a scale for infidelity. Lusting after women in your heart (*pace* Jimmy Carter) could be at one end of it, while nobbing the wife's sister and mother (as the fascist Sir Oswald Mosley almost did – in fact, he screwed his first wife's sister and their stepmother, which is close enough) would be at the other end.

In fact, though (and while I'm in judgemental mode), I reckon that coming on to the wife's daughter from a previous marriage takes some beating in the caddish stakes. And yet, statistics show that when second or subsequent marriages – in which there are stepdaughters – fall apart, the biggest cause of the end of the marriage is the stepfather trying it on with the stepdaughter.

It certainly redeems Peter Sellers (who had sex with the best friend of his wife, Ann Hayes), Roald Dahl (who left Patricia Neal, his wife of 30 years, for her best friend, Felicity 'Liccy' Crosland, whom he subsequently married) and the great womanizer Yves Montand – whom I met and found utterly charming (and who claimed, 'I think a man can have two, maybe three love affairs while he is married. But three is the absolute maximum. After that you are cheating').

There is, however, another possible answer to the question. If the 'it' refers not to cheating but to sex and emotions then, yes, it is different for men – as this wonderful gag that has been doing the email rounds illustrates perfectly.

GIRL'S DIARY – Saturday 1 July 2006

Saw John in the evening and he was acting really strangely. I went shopping in the afternoon with the girls and I did turn up a bit late so I thought it might be that. The bar was really crowded and loud so I suggested we go somewhere quieter to talk. He was still very subdued and distracted so I suggested we go somewhere nice to eat.

All through dinner he just didn't seem himself; he hardly laughed, and didn't seem to be paying any attention to me or to what I was saying. I just knew that something was wrong.

He dropped me back home and I wondered if he was going to come in; he hesitated, but followed. I asked him again if there was something the matter but he just half shook his head and turned the television on. After about 10 minutes of silence, I said I was going upstairs to bed. I put my arms around him and told him that I loved him deeply. He just gave a sigh, and a sad sort of smile. He didn't follow me up, but later he did, and I was surprised when we made love. He still seemed distant and a bit cold, and I started to think that he was going to leave me, and that he had found someone else. I cried myself to sleep.

BOY'S DIARY – Saturday 1 July 2006

England lost to Portugal on penalties. Got a shag though.

Do poofs talk like poofs because they're poofs or do they become poofs because they talk like poofs?

You either accept the premise of this question – that *some* (please note) gay men talk in an effeminate way – or you don't.

A man who immediately knew what I was on about was Simon Fanshawe, one of the founders of Stonewall, the organization that works for 'Equality & Justice For Lesbians, Gay Men & Bisexuals'.

I've known Simon – on and off – for some 16 years. Before we even met, I was a huge fan of his comedy. Nowadays, he's a successful writer and broadcaster and no longer works as a comic, but just to give you some idea of how good he was, he won the 1989 Perrier Award at Edinburgh – an award that has (so far) eluded his erstwhile co-professionals Graham Norton, Johnny Vegas, Peter Kay, Jack Dee, Eddie Izzard, Jo Brand, Alan Davies, Bill Bailey, Ross Noble and Dave Gorman.

Simon is the same age as me and comes from a similar background: indeed, the only difference between us – apart from our sexual orientation – is that he's slimmer and I've got more hair. So what did he make of my question?

'Some gay men talk like that. For them it's an unselfconscious distancing from accepted masculinity. Others talk like that because it brings with it a sense of identity. You see a similar thing with 16-year-old straight boys who are trying to be men and will talk like (straight) men do.

'The history of being gay was for so long the history of running away. With running away, you're trying to get away from the community you grew up in but you're also trying to find a new community and common ground. You're deracinating.'

You're – sorry, they're – *what*?

'Deracinating. Look it up.'

(I did – deracinate means 'To displace from one's native or accustomed environment'.)

He continued. 'You – we – were looking for men who were more feminine. Hence the voice. Hence the polari (the gay language used by Julian and Sandy in *Round The Horne*). People converged on a way of speaking, but then lots of cultures do that. Go down to Chelsea and listen to the middle classes: they converge on a common language, on a patois. Your modern poof loves all that camp because we dip in and out of it. It's a vernacular that's on my palate, or rather in my palette. It's something that men – gay and straight – can use. You should listen to yourself sometimes, Mitch. You can be a lot camper than me, you know.'

Nonsense, I replied, but the more I thought about it, the more I realized he's right. My campest friends are all (as far as I know) straight and it's certainly not my gay friends who refer to other men as 'she' and 'daughter'.

And then there are the more modern gay stereotypes of extremely butch men dressed in leather – almost as a pastiche of the masculine stereotype.

Not to mention *Brokeback Mountain*.

No, Simon's right, there's been a lot of deracinating and it has affected gay and straight culture.

But hang on, Simon, does the same go for mincing – you know, the camp, faggoty walk?

'Of course.'

All right then, here's the $64,000 question: are gays and lesbians born or made?

'Born. However, to believe there's a mono-causal reason is wrong: there isn't a single "gay" gene as the *Daily Mail* would have us believe. You should read *A Separate Creation: How Biology Makes Us Gay* by Chandler Burr. However, even if we're born and not made, there's still no need to shock your parents. When you come out, do it discreetly. At Christmas, you say to your mother, please pass the gravy to the homosexual.'

What's the origin of the 'f' word?

I'd always believed that it was an acronym – standing for 'found under carnal knowledge' – that was written on the stocks into which adulterers were placed in Ireland.

Still, I thought I'd better check. So, with no great pleasure (as readers of *Why Girls Can't Throw* will understand), I turned to linguist and philologist Dr Karen Landy.

She was as unlovely as ever – the single word 'pardon' when I asked the question speaking volumes for her low opinion of me – but once she got started, there was no stopping her.

'No, it doesn't stand for "found under carnal knowledge". Nor does it stand for "for unlawful carnal consent" or for "fornication under king's consent", nor for "forced unlawful carnal knowledge" – or indeed for any other acronym you can come up with.'

Aha, I said triumphantly, is this an example of a post-factum acronym?

'Isn't that what I just implied? In any event, the word you're searching for – and failing to find – is backronym. SOS is an example of a backronym, with people claiming it stands for "save our ship" or "save our souls" – when in fact it doesn't actually stand for anything.'

That put me in my place.

'The origin of the word is surprisingly obscure. There are similar words in Middle Dutch, Danish and Swedish dialect – meaning variously to thrust, copulate, push, strike ...'

I get the drift.

'But it is probably safest to say that the word is mainly of Germanic origin. Here, for example, is what the Oxford English Dictionary (OED) has to say on the subject: "Early modern English *fuck*, *fuk*, answering to a Middle English type *fuken* (weak verb) [which is] not found; ulterior etymology unknown. Synonymous German *ficken* can be shown to be related, as well as Dutch *fokken*, meaning *to breed*."'

Has it always been, you know, a shocking word?

'Yes. Its first known occurrence – in code because it was so shocking – was in an English poem of the late 15th century, *Flen Flyys*, that sought to poke fun at the Carmelite friars of Cambridge. The context of the usage was, "They (the friars) are not in heaven because they fuck wives of Ely."'

Fascinating.

'In fact, the word has been considered so shocking that the OED wouldn't include it in the dictionary until 1972.'

Ever since when naughty young boys have been looking it up and giggling.

'If you say so.'

Why did people think that masturbation made you blind?

Before I (attempt to) answer this question, let me just say that I entirely agree with Woody Allen, who described the old five-finger shuffle as 'sex with someone you love'. And who could disagree with Truman Capote (a tiny little tosser), who pointed out that 'the good thing about masturbation is that you don't have to dress up for it'?

In fact – and this is relevant to the question if not to the answer – I often joke that although I came to it (so to speak) late, I wanked so much between the ages of 16 and 18 that I very nearly lost my eyesight. I always say this totally seriously and (for some reason) in a Liverpudlian accent and – for a split second at least – people seem to believe me.

Well, obviously you can't go blind from too much wanking. Can you? Don't be stupid, Mitch, of course you can't! Are you sure? Yes. 100 per cent sure? Yes. Stake-the-mortgage-on-it-100-per-cent-sure? All right, let me check.

So, once again (see *Why Girls Can't Throw*), I turned to Dr Roland Powell, an MD of my acquaintance, for reassurance.

'Are you kidding me?'

Well, no, not really.

'All right then, let me put your mind at rest: there is not the slightest chance of you – or anyone else – losing their eyesight as a result of excessive masturbation.'

What, even if one were wanking while crossing the road?

He ignored my idiotic attempt at witticism. 'In fact, the only possible adverse consequence of excessive masturbation would be chafed and sore genitalia.'

As we were talking, I found myself singing The Vapors' song 'Turning Japanese' which is reckoned to be about the joys of self-abuse because men screw their eyes up – thereby making them look Japanese – as they reach the vinegar strokes (or 'climax'). Perhaps, I suggested to the good doctor, this explains the fears about blindness?

'I'm not sure I follow your train of logic but it's clear that those fears were stoked by misguided people who were desperate to stop boys from masturbating.'

I did some further research into this and came across a doctor named Samuel August Tissot who, in 1760, wrote *'L'Onanisme, ou Dissertation Physique sur les Maladies Produites par la Masturbation'* (you can translate it yourself). This cheerful little tome – which was still being published in the 20th century – aimed to scare generations of adolescent boys into sleeping with their hands above the sheets. Here's Tissot writing about a home visit he made to a poor fellow supposedly suffering from 'post-masturbation disease'.

I went to his home; what I found was less a living being than a cadaver lying on straw, thin, pale, exuding a loathsome stench, almost incapable of movement. A pale and watery blood often dripped from his nose, he drooled continually; subject to attacks of diarrhea, he defecated in his bed without noticing it; there was constant flow of semen; his eyes, sticky, blurry, dull, had lost all power of movement; his pulse was extremely weak and racing; labored respiration, extreme emaciation, except for the feet, which were showing signs of edema. Mental disorder was equally evident; without ideas, without memory, incapable of linking two sentences, without reflection, without fear of his fate, lacking all feeling except that of pain, which returned at least every three days with each new attack. Thus sunk below the level of the beast, a spectacle of unimaginable horror, it was difficult to believe that he had once belonged to the human race. ... He died after several weeks, in June 1757, his entire body covered in edemas.

And all that just from too much time spent playing the pink oboe.

As a result of scaremongering by Tissot (or 'Tosser Tissot' as we call him round my way) and others like him, there was plenty of interest in 'cures' to stop youths from abusing themselves. Dr Benjamin Rush, a signatory to the US Declaration of Independence, recommended 'a vegetable diet, temperance, bodily labor, cold baths, avoidance of obscenity, music, a close study of mathematics, military glory, and, if all else failed, castor oil'.

John Harvey Kellogg, the cereal manufacturer, was dead set against masturbation which (or so he believed) caused idleness, abnormal sexual passions, gluttony and sedentary employment.

Sounds about right.

Kellogg – sorry, Dr Kellogg – said of masturbation: 'The most loathsome reptile, rolling in the slush and slime of its stagnant pool, would not demean itself', and believed that a bowl of Corn Flakes would help to take a young man's mind off it.

If that didn't work, Kellogg favoured the use of an electrical urethral probe in 15-minute doses, two or three times a week. He also made use of the 'bougie', a long, flexible tube made of rubber or metal that was inserted into the male urethra, often delivering a caustic dose of burnt alum or silver nitrate or some other noxious substance.

Kellogg also recommended bandaging boys' genitals, and/or tying their hands to the bedposts at night.

Other contemporary deterrents included the application of leeches to the inner thighs, confinement in straitjackets, wrappings of cold, wet sheets while sleeping, burning genital tissue with a hot iron, metal gloves, infibulation, urethral rings of metal spikes that would stab the penis if it became erect and various anti-masturbation contraptions like the genital cage that used springs to hold a boy's penis and scrotum in place and the device that sounded an alarm if a boy had an erection. If all else failed, there was always castration.

Girls weren't excluded. There were metal vulva guards and, just to be safe, clitoridectomies (a disgusting practice still carried out in parts of Africa).

By comparison with those, other supposed cures – like potassium bromide, hot pepper, hydrochloric acid or mercury – seem relatively civilized, but perhaps not as much fun as the opium or marijuana that some boys were given to take their minds off masturbation.

Mind you, it was difficult for them to avoid thinking about it – especially as Victorian parents would take their children to wax museums just to see the gruesome 'effects' of post-masturbation disease.

Meanwhile, schools were equipped with anti-masturbation benches designed so that a young man's thighs were not brushed together in a way that might excite him. This was not altogether stupid: in a previous scientific volume I have referred to the phenomenon of the 'class wanker' and it's entirely possible that such a contraption might have deterred him. In fact, it wouldn't have deterred *our* class wanker, who was totally undeterrable and, indeed, indefatigable, but it might have stopped André Gide, the French author, who was expelled from school for wanking in class.

This obsession with – against – masturbation can perhaps be explained by the Victorians' belief that we only had a limited amount of semen which shouldn't be wasted but should be saved for our wives to make the sons and daughters who would run the Empire. These Victorians believed that this reservoir of cum was located at the base of the spine. Obviously, they were absolutely tonto but you can see what led them to believe that that was where it would be, as every time a man ejaculates, he feels a spasm in just that place. Well, this man does anyway.

In fact, the conviction that there was a set number of ejaculations for each man persisted well into the 20th century. Ernest Hemingway, for example, earnestly (*sic*) declared, 'The number of available orgasms is fixed at birth and can be expended. A young man should make love very seldom or he will have nothing left for middle age.'

Er, no.

Looking back, it seems extraordinary the lengths to which otherwise intelligent men went just to stop boys doing what comes naturally, but I guess it has to be seen in the context of a repressed age in which *any* form of self-indulgence or self-expression was frowned upon – to the extent that *any* abuse justified the prevention of self-abuse.

Is bestiality immoral?

Absent-mindedly, I Googled the three words of the question and got just four results but one of them was very interesting: in a blog site named the daily kos, a man called Neil Sinhababu posed just that question. I contacted him and obtained his permission to share the results with you.

He wrote: 'I've never thought there was anything immoral about a human being having sex with a nonhuman animal. Not that I'd ever do that sort of thing, but if I found that someone I knew had done it, my feelings would be more of surprised amusement than of moral disapprobation. I'm curious about what other people think about this.'

He went on to qualify this by writing: 'I'm talking about cases of bestiality where there isn't any harm to either the animal or the human being, and both parties have a good time. Let's also consider cases where no new diseases make the jump across species as a result of the sexual encounter.

'As a utilitarian about morality, I think that actions are good in virtue of their promoting the general happiness and decreasing suffering, and bad in virtue of their decreasing happiness or increasing the amount of suffering in the world. (Complications arise when people intend good things, but bad things result, and vice versa. But this can be kept aside from the bestiality issue.) Utilitarianism is compatible with my view on the bestiality case, since I think the possibility of pleasure and the absence of harm mean that sex with animals is OK. However, I imagine that most people disapprove of bestiality in a way that utilitarianism can't account for.'

After reading such a mature, intelligent, philosophical argument, you'll be as surprised as I (and, no doubt, Neil too) was that out of the 106 people who voted, a whopping 92 people thought it was immoral, seven were unsure and only another seven people thought there wasn't 'something morally wrong about a person having sex with an animal'.

For my own part, I admire Neil's utilitarian argument but I would vote with the majority because, as Neil concedes, utilitarianism doesn't cover this issue. Indeed, it was Jeremy Bentham (the father of utilitarianism himself) who, realizing that utilitarianism couldn't be applied to animals, said instead, 'The point is not how clever they are but do they feel pain, can they suffer?'

On the grounds of suffering, there's no evidence to suggest that bestiality is any worse for an animal than, say, intensive farming followed by a trip to the abattoir: indeed it is almost certainly preferable.

Which leaves us with the human participants. As you know, my general approach to matters of sex is: whatever consenting adults consent to do in private. With bestiality, one has to ask how informed and reasonable the consent is. Now add to the mix the undeniable fact that bestial images are widely used in pornography with the clear intention of demeaning the human (invariably a woman) and I would say that the whole issue becomes tainted to such an extent so as to render bestiality itself – even in the abstract – immoral.

There is one qualification to this. If bestiality is sex with animals, zoophilia is (or so its practitioners would have it) love – albeit sexual love – with animals. I understand the distinction but would still maintain that inter-species sex is 'a bad thing'.

Fortunately, human–animal couplings are rare. However, I can tell you that the porn star Linda Lovelace had sex with a dog for a porn film, that Algernon Swinburne used to do it with his pet monkey (which he later killed and ate when it bit one of his guests) and that Larry Flynt had a sexual experience (in 1948) with a chicken which he wrote about in his book *Sex, Lies, & Politics: The Naked Truth*.

Can open marriages work?

Like most people, I've a tendency to universalize my own experience – especially when that experience is germane. So let me start my answer by saying that I've been happily married for 22 years but that a big reason for my – our (I hope) – marital happiness is that it's a monogamous relationship. Before meeting Penny (my wife), the longest I ever lived with a woman was for 48 hours – and that was only because I put my back out. Pre-Penny, I was, to put it mildly, a bit of a toe-rag; since then, I've been a one-woman man (in deed if not always in thought). It's not a question of fidelity (a much overrated virtue: give me loyalty or, better still, kindness any day) for the sake of fidelity but because, for me, fooling around would be the thin end of the wedge. As the late Richard Burton said, 'The minute you start fiddling around outside the idea of monogamy, nothing satisfies any more.' I'm pretty sure that's how it would be for me.

And yet it would be foolish to pretend that there's only one path to happiness – especially as, according to anthropologists, the survival of the species is predicated on men scattering their seed far and wide. After all, as Somerset Maugham pointed out, 'You know, of course, that the Tasmanians, who never committed adultery, are now extinct.'

Some men even go so far as to claim that the desire to sleep with as many women as possible is hardwired into the male psyche. I can remember George Burns saying, 'If you were married to Marilyn Monroe – you'd cheat with some ugly girl.'

As we've already established, a woman has a different anthropological imperative: she needs to find a man who will nurture and provide for her and her baby. Interestingly, this might not be the same man who made her pregnant in the first place. The evidence suggests that a woman seeks the biggest alpha male (aka the biggest bastard) to impregnate her and then the most suitable man to look after her and the baby. Inevitably, in modern society, she tries to find a man who combines both qualities but her primeval need to keep her man runs deep.

So with women programmed to cheat before becoming mothers and men programmed to cheat after becoming fathers, it's a wonder the divorce rate isn't even greater than one in three (like three in three). The fact that it isn't is a tribute to love, trust and the human ability to shake off atavistic conditioning.

In this context, an open marriage could seem less like a total indulgence and more like a sophisticated arrangement to safeguard the structure – albeit not the substance – of marriage.

My friend Tim and his wife, Jill, have an open marriage. Although Tim and Jill miss very few opportunities to bang on about their – yawn – love lives, I have changed their names for the sake of their children (one of whom is just 12 years old). They've been 'open' for over two years and they say that far from damaging their relationship, it's actually enhanced it. They even go to swinging parties together and swap partners. Personally, I can't think of anything more ghastly but they seem to thrive on it – or, at least, Jill does. Because just as it's rare to find two people in a marriage with precisely the same sex drive, so too is it unlikely that both partners will have the same desire to open up their relationship to outsiders. Consequently, in every open marriage, there has to be an instigator. Ordinarily, for obvious reasons, it's the man but, in this instance, it was Jill's idea. After discovering that Tim had had a one-night stand while working away from home, she decided to get even by shagging the architect who was doing their extension. Apparently, she enjoyed it so much that she told Tim that that way lay their marital salvation. It seems to work for them, though I have my doubts. For starters, they're far too evangelical about it: you know, 'come on in, the water's lovely!' (and no, I don't think they're trying to tap us up personally) and, secondly, the time will surely come when either a) one of them – most probably Tim – will decide that, like Mrs Patrick Campbell, they yearn for 'the deep, deep peace of the double bed after the hurly burly of the chaise longue' (you'll note that I have a somewhat romanticized view of adultery) or b) one of them – most probably Jill – will find someone who represents more than just a quick lay and will split up the marriage to go off with that person.

Who knows? Meanwhile, they're both getting plenty of great sex. So who's the idiot?

The fact is that many couples have or had open marriages. Here's a partial list:

Aneurin Bevan & Jennie Lee

Camilla & Andrew Parker Bowles

Harold & Grace Robbins

Bertrand Russell & Dora Black

Terry & Alison Jones

Carl & Emma Jung

John F. & Jacqueline Kennedy

Leonard & Virginia Woolf

William & Jane Morris

Salvador & Gala Dali

Harold Nicolson & Vita Sackville-West

Lord Louis & Lady Edwina Mountbatten

George & Diana Melly

Dmitri & Nina Shostakovich

Havelock & Edith Ellis

Jay & Fran Landesman

David & Angie Bowie

Gary & Veronica (Rocky) Cooper

Sir William & Lady Emma Hamilton

Horatio & Fanny Nelson

Marlene Dietrich & Rudolf Sieber

Lyndon & Lady Bird Johnson

What conclusions can we draw from this list (other than that I'm a damn fine researcher – and more than a little strange)? Some of the marriages survived, some thrived, some died. Perhaps, opening up the marriage postponed the death rites in that last category. But what do you notice about nearly all of these names? Yup, they're mostly all dead. This isn't entirely due to my healthy respect for the laws of libel. It's because I suspect that the whole question of open marriages harks back to the days when marriage itself was *de rigueur* and divorce was too stigmatic and expensive to contemplate. Now that people can and do 'live in sin' and have multiple sequential partners without attracting very much adverse comment, who needs an open marriage?

If I decide to become a slave to a dominatrix, who pays whom?

The clue to the answer is in the question: if I decide ...

Obviously, if it's something I want to do, I'm going to have to pay for it. But why would I pay to be someone's slave? Surely the whole point of slavery is that one is owned – not that one pays to be owned? Doesn't that upset the delicate balance of the master–slave relationship? I mean, how would the slave trade of the 18th century have operated if slaves had to pay their masters? Simon Legree would have been out of work (no bad thing).

I'm fortunate enough to strike gold with the first dominatrix I find: Mistress Mia, who has a listing that reads:

I Mistress Mia am looking for a special little slave, you will look after my every need in the house, you will take me shopping and whatever i demand of you. if you can not stay fri to sun then dont bother, if you can what are you waiting for slave mistress wonts to here from you. call me on ...

So I called her and told her about this book and asked the question.

She laughed. 'They pay me!'

How much?

'£120 an hour.'

Not for the whole weekend, surely?

'No, obviously it's less for the whole weekend.'

But even so, that's an awful lot of money just to do your shopping and carry out your demands. Sounds to me like any married man's regular Saturday morning.

She giggled.

I was about to ask the $64,000 question – or maybe that should be the £120 question – why do they do it? Then suddenly I realized that I knew why they did it. It's about control issues and working through fantasies, isn't it?

Mistress Mia confirmed that it was. 'There are a lot of men out there who …' Her voice trailed off but I caught her drift.

For some reason, I felt ashamed. No, it wasn't 'some reason'. Here I was again, making fun of other people's needs/problems/outlets. Just because I have no personal need for Mistress Mia doesn't mean I should deride those who do.

We talked for quite a lot longer. She's a fine woman (mid-40s, I should say) who is tolerant (and sometimes fond) of her clients. 'I'm a dominant woman by nature. I'm very assertive and men just love that. And the older I get the more assertive I get.'

Good point: being a dominatrix means never having to say you're retiring. The older a dom gets, presumably the more appealing she'll be – at least to some blokes.

I looked her up again on the internet.

> hello slaves and all u subs, on ur knees before ur goddess, good, now i session in dover wed and sat 11 to 11. i have use of a fully equipped dungeon. i cater for most fetishes, cp and bodyworship. so come crawl to a goddess and let me kiss ur lips and enter ur soul

OK, so her grammar and syntax aren't up to much – but she certainly gets her message across.

And while I might not care for being corporally punished in a dungeon (however well equipped) – indeed, I would pay good money NOT to be so treated – it's evident that there are several men who do. You might even be one of them.

Good luck to them and, if appropriate, to you too.

We know that men become women but do any women become men?
(And does acquiring a penis help them to understand the offside rule?)

I am privileged to number among my friends a fine young man named Bryn ... who used to be a fine young woman named Bee.

Anyway, Bryn tells me that there are probably as many transsexual men (that's women who become or live as men) as there are transsexual women (men who become or live as women). However, when it comes to medical treatment – including drugs and operations – transsexual women outnumber transsexual men. Having said that, in Poland, the majority of sex-change operations are female-to-male rather than male-to-female.

According to Bryn, 'The main reason why relatively few transsexual men have medical help to live as men is because, in our society, it's much easier for a woman to lead the life of a man than it is for a man to lead the life of a woman.'

While I pride myself on my tolerance, I confess that I'm not – how can I put it? – the most metrosexual of men. Sometimes I feel like that Harry Enfield character, the father who struggles to come to terms with his gay son and is forever putting his foot in it, but I've had no difficulty whatsoever accepting Bee as Bryn.

I think it's because although 'she' wasn't especially butch, her squat shapeless body combined with a severely cropped hairstyle made her look an improbable woman. Having said that, she always had a beautiful voice, which, fortunately for him, is still very fine (albeit in a lower register). When she told me that she was becoming a man, I wasn't really very surprised. In truth, I felt relieved.

You see, Bee was a lesbian and although I had absolutely no problem with that (my stepsister is also a lesbian), I always felt I had to watch what I said. This wasn't because Bee was at all touchy – *au contraire* – but because, even at the best of times, I can come across as a potty-mouthed oaf. Consequently, not only was I careful never to refer to lesbians as 'lezzers' or 'dykes' (words that, in any event, rarely pass my lips) but I also had to modify my – ahem – somewhat misogynistic views.

Conversations with Bee could never start with lines like 'Women, huh!' or 'Bloody women, can't live with them, can't shoot them'.

In short, there was an element of treading on eggshells.

Then Bee gave me the news … and suddenly, I could say what I liked! And you can be sure I did.

Bryn, however, is much more measured and civilized than I am. Although, as a convert (as it were), he might be expected to embrace his new gender so wholeheartedly that he ends up as a stereotypical 'lad' or he-man, he is, in truth, no different from how he was as a woman: a thoroughly decent human being. Although, journalistic integrity compels me to report that he did recently point out to me that one should never trust any creature that bleeds for a week every month without dying.

The differences between Bee and Bryn are much more subtle than one might have expected: he looks much more impressive as a man than as a woman, and although he has maintained the same weight (less the weight of his breasts), he looks so much slimmer and fitter. There's also the sense – or, at least, this is what I've inferred – that he's much happier in his own skin.

In short, Bryn is a top bloke.

But, to answer the second part of the original question, does he understand the offside position any better as a man than he did as a woman?

Er, no.

'I learned all I know about the offside rule from *Bend It Like Beckham*,' says Bryn with a big smile on his face (which currently boasts a fine stubble).

And you saw that …

'As a woman. So, no, I don't understand it any better now.'

I told him he was a big girl's blouse (something you can call a man but not a woman and certainly not a lesbian).

'Well, maybe, but I'm a huge rugby union fan – always have been.'

Like I say, top bloke.

... And following on from that: when a lesbian has a sex-change operation to become a man, does her erstwhile lesbian partner cease to be a lesbian?

Once again, I'm fortunate enough to have Bryn as an expert guide.

As Bee, he lived in a lesbian relationship with Sarah.

Now that Sarah is living with a man in a sexual relationship, has she become, *ipso facto*, heterosexual?

'No,' says Bryn, clearly enjoying the intellectual challenge of the conundrum (see, he really is a man!). 'She's still a lesbian. The fact that she was in love with Bee and is now in love with Bryn doesn't reflect a change on her part but on mine. I'm the one who's changed, not her.'

But still ...

'Yes, I know what you're saying. Put it this way, she loves me – well, hopefully anyway. That's me, Bee, Bryn or whatever label you want to put on me. I'm essentially the same person I always was – whatever my gender.'

That's fair enough.

'And the point is that if we ever split up—'

Perish the thought.

'Absolutely. Sarah would still be a lesbian and would, no doubt, get together with another woman.'

I understand, I told him.

And, incredible as it might sound, I really do.

Has any man ever gone to a prostitute and found someone he knew?

That's got to be a nightmare, no? Fellow goes to a prostitute and finds his wife/sister/wife's sister – well, you fill in your own unbelievably horrid scenario. One thing's for certain, it would lead to instant detumescence. No matter how much Viagra you might have swallowed.

I asked around – checked with the usual suspects – but drew a complete blank. In fact, none of my crowd even admitted to having ever been with a prostitute – let alone found one he already knew.

This is manifestly absurd. There are so many tarts in this country that, by the laws of probability, some of my mates must have flashed the cash. And don't let the denials that 'I'm a happily married man' fool you: I remember being accosted by a pimp in Soho a few years ago. As he tried to interest me in the photos in his folder (those were the days before mobile phones/cameras), I protested that I was – yes – 'a happily married man'.

'Happily married?' he said, his face breaking into a big grin. 'If it wasn't for married men, I wouldn't have any clients.'

So there.

Nor is prostitution uniquely rife in Britain. In the US, it is estimated that 23 people in 100,000 are prostitutes (or 0.023 per cent of the population). Not an insignificant number.

Anyway, having failed so miserably with my friends, I logged on to the fabulously comprehensive site of www.punternet.com. What an eye-opener! You should go there – if only to read the 'field reports' which are (evidently) so well researched and, for the most part, well written that they would put consumer journalists to shame.

Perhaps the most extraordinary thing that the site reveals is the prevalence of prostitution in Britain. I mean, you'd expect to find it in

London and in the major cities – but in Amersham? Harrogate? Worthing (aka God's waiting-room by the sea)?

Alas, even after reading hundreds of reports, I hadn't found anyone who'd got the shock of their lives (I guess they wouldn't exactly rush to write about it if they had).

So I logged on to some of the (very) many chat rooms devoted to prostitution – home and abroad – and ran into a very different problem: the assumption that I was a wanker.

All right, so I am but not in that sense. The questions I was asking were genuine – as you must surely concur. Trouble was, no one – neither the girls nor their clients – believed me. And the more I protested my innocence, that I was a professional writer, the more they told me, 'Go away, tosser.'

But I'm Mitchell Symons, the author of *Why Girls Can't Throw*, just go to Amazon and look me up!

'How do we know you're him? You're probably making it up.'

But obviously I'm him – me – why on earth would I pretend to be him – me? It beggars belief!

Therefore, in the interests of research – honest! – I decided to pay a visit to a brothel and talk to a professional, face-to-face. It's what we in the writing biz call 'fact-finding' and perfectly valid – even if I did have the devil's own job explaining it to my wife who, not unreasonably, asked me why I was insisting on a primary source for this question when I was perfectly happy using secondary and tertiary sources for all the others ('nicking it off the internet' were her precise words, as I recall).

Having looked up a likely brothel (in all but name) in the local paper, I drove to a rundown part of Brighton, parked and found myself outside a grotty house.

The middle-aged woman who answered the door was wearing a badly fitting tracksuit and leggings. With a voice that betrayed a lifetime's devotion to cigarettes, she bade me come inside. Blimey, I thought, if she's one of 'em, I'd rather go with Lorena Bobbitt. What's that line in *Saving Private Ryan*? 'She fell off an ugly tree and hit every branch on the way down?' Yup, that was her.

But it turned out that she was only the maid and, I later concluded, probably a former prostitute herself. Not what you'd call a walking testament to the benefits of a life on the game.

I looked around the dingy room into which she'd ushered me, asking me to wait while she rounded up all the spare girls and sent them in for my perusal. The room wasn't what you'd call over-furnished: queen-sized bed, bedside table with a box of tissues and a broken lampstand, wooden chair and a chest of drawers with a stack of top-shelf magazines on it – all well thumbed through by the look of it. In the corner was an open wardrobe where I could see a number of uniforms from the stock list of (supposed) male fantasies – nurse, schoolgirl, policewoman.

A girl wearing a negligee knocked and entered the room. Well, I say a girl, she was 35 if she was a day: overweight, bad skin and not much prettier than the maid. She'd be lucky to give it away, I thought, while simultaneously chiding myself for my lack of charity.

'My name's Candy,' she said, in a surprisingly posh accent, and left the room.

The next girl was again overweight but she had a decent cleavage. 'I'm Layla,' she said, offering me her hand. It somehow seemed an incongruous greeting in what was, after all, a whorehouse.

The third girl – Zoe – was young (23, as I later discovered), attractive and looked extremely fetching in a black basque. I decided to pick her, not, if I was being honest, because she would have a wealth of experience to draw upon but because I didn't think it was inconsistent with either my mission or, indeed, my marriage vows (not that I took any as we were married in a register office) to talk with an attractive girl for a few minutes.

There was no one else available – the other three of the six girls I had been promised on the phone when I had called for the address were presumably busy – and so I told the maid that I'd like to see Zoe.

'So what would you like?' asked Zoe.

'Can we just talk?'

'Sure,' she replied, although I could see her thinking, 'We've got a right one here.'

'No, seriously. I'm writing a book – it's the follow-up to my last book, *Why Girls Can't Throw*—'

'I can.'

'What?'

'Throw! I can throw.'

'Ah yes, quite possibly. In fact, I answer that question in the book, and it turns out that girls can indeed throw when they've been taught.' I suddenly remembered where I was. 'So what would you charge for your time?'

'Well, if you really want to talk, I'll charge you £40 for 30 minutes. Is that OK?'

I handed over the money and she disappeared, to return a couple of minutes later.

'Where do you want me?'

'I don't mind,' I spluttered. 'Perhaps if I sit in the chair and you sit on the bed?'

'All right.'

And then she started to peel off her basque. 'Excuse me!'

'Yes?' she said, with her really rather excellent breasts on display.

I was torn between not wanting to appear censorious and not wanting to be an old lech. Well, which do you think won? And so I asked her whether she'd ever met anyone she already knew in her capacity as a …

'Working girl.'

'Yes, as a working girl.'

It turned out that she hadn't – partly because she wasn't from Brighton – but that her friend Emma, a local girl, had entertained a man she subsequently met at a family gathering.

'And was it embarrassing?'

'No, not for her. She wasn't the one who was married. But he nearly had a nervous breakdown on the spot!'

'How would you feel if it happened to you?'

She tilted her head to one side and gave it some thought. 'I dunno. I mean, I'm married but my husband knows what I do.'

I was intrigued to discover she was married. 'How come he doesn't mind?'

'We need the money and he doesn't earn very much.'

'But doesn't it, er, have an adverse effect on your relationship?'

'Nah.'

There wasn't much I could reply to that and so I asked her more about herself and her work, taking notes in my (extremely poor) shorthand as she spoke – only occasionally looking up to catch a glimpse of her … well, never mind what, let's just say that sometimes there are some perks to my work.

'Trick is to make the punter relax – be pleasant to him – and he'll be nice back. Sometimes it's over in seconds and then you've earned 40 quid for a minute's work. Where else could you get that much? And it's tax-free. At my last place, I made 340 quid in one night. Now that's good money.

'I don't do anal,' she said apropos of nothing. 'Some of the girls do but I don't. I also don't do French without a condom. It's not because I'm squeamish or anything, it's because I'm frightened of getting chlamydia.'

'Can you get it like that?'

'Yes. You get it from unprotected sex. It doesn't do anything to you at the time but it can make you infertile later on. I've told one or two of the other girls at the other place I work about it and they've stopped doing any unprotected sex – except maybe breast relief.

'I go to a clinic regularly where they know I'm a working girl and they give me priority. It isn't just chlamydia, there's also genital warts. They're contagious too. You can't be too careful.'

Hmm … not quite the conversation I'd imagined. 'Tell me,' I said, 'do you derive any pleasure from your work?'

She smiled – possibly at my attempt at lofty detachment.

'Do you mean have I ever come? Yeah, once or twice.'

We exchanged a few more pleasantries and then the time was up and we were shaking hands. 'Come back and ask for me,' she said, leaving me in no doubt what she meant.

I pretended to misunderstand her. 'It's OK, I've got everything I want.'

* * * *

So that's the question answered – sort of – and a few others besides. One thing my (albeit) limited experience did give me was a respect for prostitutes – or at least *that* prostitute (if not for prostitution): an understanding that they're human too and not just toys for boys.

One final thought on the question. There are plenty of men who have gone to prostitutes and discovered that they (the pros) know them (the punters). Those are, of course, the ones who find themselves on the front pages of the tabloid press. But they're not alone. The following men all had sex with prostitutes – some of them have even boasted about it: Elvis Presley, Charlie Chaplin, Duke Ellington, Vincent van Gogh, Clark Gable, Jean-Paul Sartre, Errol Flynn, Victor Hugo, John Keats,

Henri de Toulouse-Lautrec, Oscar Wilde (who contracted syphilis from one when at university), Georges Simenon, Casanova, Honoré de Balzac, Johannes Brahms, Lord Byron, Fyodor Dostoevsky, King Edward VII, F. Scott Fitzgerald, George Gershwin, Ernest Hemingway, Friedrich Nietzsche, Grigori Rasputin, Hans Christian Andersen (who used to go to brothels to *talk* with the girls), Dudley Moore, Diego Maradona (who ordered 20 prostitutes to be sent up to his room at the Dorchester and then had sex with one of them), Al Capone and Keith Moon.

In addition, the following men all lost their virginity with prostitutes: Henry Fonda, David Niven, Anton Chekhov, the Duke of Windsor, Napoleon Bonaparte, James Boswell, James Joyce, John F. Kennedy (the girl charged $3), Benito Mussolini, Leo Tolstoy, H.G. Wells, Groucho Marx, Frank Skinner and Ilie Nastase.

I couldn't find any women who'd lost their virginity with male prostitutes but the following men all paid for sex with male prostitutes or rent boys and some of them were 'outed' as punters by them: Mark Oaten, Sir Arthur C. Clarke, George Cukor, Howard Hughes, A.E. Housman, Charles Laughton, Joe Orton, Leonardo da Vinci, Monty Woolley, Cole Porter, Pier Paolo Pasolini, T.E. Lawrence, Russell Harty, Cecil Beaton, Errol Flynn, W. Somerset Maugham, Montgomery Clift, André Gide, Christopher Isherwood, Yukio Mishima, Oscar Wilde, Lord Alfred Douglas and Brian Epstein.

... And why do prostitutes offer French but not Danish?

French is, as we know, oral sex, while Danish is short for Danish pastries.

I didn't ask Zoe whether she offered Danish but having seen the shabby surroundings of her workplace I very much doubt it.

There are a lot of silly questions in this book that manage to provoke really rather interesting answers.

I don't think this is one of them.

Obviously, there is a certain amount of fun to be had with euphemisms but it's all a bit old hat. The days when prostitutes would advertise 'French lessons' or put up cards saying 'Model seeks unusual positions' are long gone. Nowadays, it's much more in your face – whether it's on the internet or on a card in a telephone box.

Maybe directness is a good thing – though not, I'd have thought, if kids could trip over them.

Taking the question at face value, I was surprised to see just how much some of the brothels (in all but name) offer on their websites. Jacuzzi baths, drinks, showers – who knows? Maybe you can get pastries as well.

The thing to remember is that prostitution is capitalism at its rawest and most unfettered: whatever a person's prepared to do in return for what another person's prepared to pay.

It may be ugly – and, at the bottom end of the market, where girls are lured from Eastern Europe and then effectively kept as sex slaves, it undoubtedly is. However, whatever free adult citizens choose to get up to in private isn't anyone else's business but theirs.

I asked one punter I found online why he paid for sex and he told me that he had girlfriends but that he preferred going with tarts. 'Apart from anything, it's cheaper,' he said, echoing the old saying that the big difference between sex for money and sex for free is that sex for money usually costs less. In other words, with prostitutes, men are paying for the sex and the privilege of not having to undergo post-coital intimacies. Or, as they say in Hollywood, you don't pay a whore to come, you pay her to go.

Does the etiquette of swinging extend to asking your mate's wife if she'll iron your shirt?

I've already shared with you my opinions on 'open marriages' so you won't be too surprised to learn that Mrs S and I don't go in for wife-swapping or, as it's sometimes known, swinging. Besides, it wouldn't be fair: the man who got my wife would be a hell of lot luckier than his missus would be (notwithstanding my fascinating personality, I am more mattress than man).

Which was why I was extremely lucky to find Dave and Linda, a couple who organize, er, get-togethers at their house in East Sussex (http://www.skinnydippersuk.com/index2.html).

Dave looks like Peter Stringfellow's (not so) younger brother, while Linda, his partner of some 14 years, looks – I can think of no better word – fit.

The first thing Dave corrects me on is my terminology. 'We don't like the word "swinging", we prefer "adult parties". But our parties are not just about sex. If you go to a party where you don't fancy people, it's boring. We come from the music scene so we just took that scene into this scene. There's no pressure.

'We do it because we believe in it. It's a private house, which cuts through the club stuff. We're not technically restrained by anything. We like to party. There's not much money in it but obviously you have to stay in business.

'I grew up in the sixties. I try to create an atmosphere of freedom. The golden rule is: so long as a couple goes home together.

Don't come here if you're in trouble. You've got more chance of losing your partner at Tesco's—'

Not at our local branch, I mutter.

'—than you have at one of our parties. If someone does lose their partner at one of our parties, they would have done so anyway.'

That sounds as though you're denying any cause and effect between swinging – sorry, 'partying' – and splitting up.

'Coming into this scene can show up the flaws in a relationship and it accelerates them. People who come along have flaws and this might be a way of working through.'

Hmm.

And then, blow me down – stop tittering there at the back – Dave and Linda invite me to come along.

What, on my own?

'On your own or with your wife.'

Gulp.

'Have a look at some of the people on the website.'

I did and they all – or mostly all – looked perfectly normal. Whatever normal means.

'Look, we get between 100 and 180 people at our parties. Mostly couples but also singles. Friday nights, we have singles as well as couples.'

Mostly men, these singles?

'No, there isn't a surplus of men.'

Another cherished myth exploded.

It's tempting – it was – but it's not really me.

'Sure?'

NO! But I'm sticking with that. Besides, Dave and Linda, with all this super information you're giving me, you're neatly managing to evade the question: I know that at one of your parties, a man can proposition a woman – and vice versa – but what if he were to ask her to iron his shirt?

Understandably, Dave and Linda were somewhat less forthcoming on this (hitherto unexplored) aspect of adult partying and I was starting to feel like every sort of silly ass when an extraordinary thought occurred to me: ask an impertinent question and you're halfway to finding a pertinent answer.

Of course I had meant the question to be silly and facetious but, in fact, there's an important truth in there: if you reduce sexual intercourse, the ultimate act of intimacy, to the level of a parlour game to be played with multiple partners, then you need to find something else to replace it. And, who knows, performing minor chores for each other might be all that you've got left.

Having said that, each to their own, and East Sussex is tantalizingly close to where I live …

Why do men fall asleep after sex?

Well, I do. Don't all men? Why? Presumably because we have sex last thing at night. Also, as men, we're task-orientated: job done, let's move on to the next one, which, after a good fart, is going to sleep. The cuddle can wait for another day.

Having said that, it is undoubtedly true that sex – accompanied or solo – does make you sleepy.

Is there a cause and effect?

I decided to ask Dr Roland Powell, my pet MD, who told me that he has actually had (female) patients complain to him about this.

Why doesn't he just tell them to get a life?

'I would, but don't forget that I am a private GP.'

'Nuff said. So what causes men's sleepiness after sex?

'Well, there's a lot in what you say about having sex just before you go to sleep and therefore feeling sleepy – especially if there's been some exertion to help to release natural endorphins that relax us.

'You'll also find that, just before and during orgasm, you experience a quicker heart rate and higher blood pressure. After orgasm, the heart rate slows and the blood pressure drops and both of those are conducive to sleep.

'But that's not all. An orgasm – male or female – also releases oxytocin, which is the same hormone that's released when women are breastfeeding and it's designed to put babies to sleep. Obviously, it has the same effect on adults. Yes, and that means women too.'

Is it possible to 'enlarge your penis'?

Consider the following joke:

> A man is in his favourite (expensive) restaurant when he notices a beautiful woman sitting all alone at a nearby table. He calls the waiter and asks for their most expensive bottle of Champagne to be sent over to her. The waiter does this and the woman sends a note to the man that reads: 'For me to accept this bottle, you need to have a Mercedes in your garage, a million dollars in the bank, and seven inches in your pants.' After reading her note, the man sends back a note of his own: 'Just to let you know, I have a Rolls Royce in my garage, twenty million dollars in the bank, but not even for a woman as beautiful as you would I cut off three inches. So please send back the bottle.'

OK, first off, here are the facts. According to Gebhard and Johnson (1979), the average erect penis of males in the US is 5–7 inches long and the average circumference is 4–6 inches.

So what can the man who is below average, or above average but desperately insecure, do? Alas, it turns out, not much at all.

If a chap's lost (almost all of) his penis in – say – a bacon-slicer moment, then there is the possibility of reconstructive surgery. However, this is an incredibly intricate and laborious medical procedure and is simply not appropriate for purely cosmetic purposes.

Then there are silicon rods which are inserted to help men with erectile dysfunction but a flaccid dick is not the same as a small one. There's really not a lot that can be done.

So what is one to make of all the advice available on the internet? I mean, not many days go by when I don't receive an invitation to enlarge my penis. Offers of patches, hypnosis, exercisers, pills, pumps and something called an extender device (least said, soonest groin ache mended) have all entered my in-box. Oh yes, and surgery.

But hang on a second, Mitch, didn't you just say that surgery wasn't – what was the word you used? – 'appropriate'?

Yes, but that doesn't stop people offering it and, presumably, people taking them up on it. Desperate people will do almost anything. And looking at some of the (before) pictures on such websites, I think we might have to redefine the meaning of the word 'desperate'. I have seen bigger penises on an Action Man doll.

Mind you, even the after pictures – presumably touched up (if you get my drift) – aren't that impressive. Who could be bothered? Wouldn't it be cheaper – and less painful – to buy a fast car?

To be fair to the companies offering enlargement surgery – though there's no reason why one should, given that it could be argued that they're trading in (and taking advantage of) people's miserable insecurity – they can make a tiny difference by adding a little fat to increase the length or girth, but we are talking tiny (before and after).

Still, there's clearly a market out there. Put 'increase the size of your penis' as a specific phrase into Google and see how many hits you get. I got 36,000 and nearly all of those were ads.

Pills seem to be the preferred method – 100 PER CENT GUARANTEED!!! – and while they might have the teensiest effect on teensy todgers (surely not every claim is a lie?), their efficacy would seem to be limited – or else every underendowed bloke would be taking them.

What's the best/worst pick-up line?

Regular readers of my books – and a big hello to you both – might remember that I ran a list of chat-up lines in *This Book*.

Here are some of them:

- You don't know me but I dreamt about you last night.
- Did it hurt when you fell from heaven?
- If I could rearrange the alphabet, I'd put U and I together.
- Can I buy you a drink or do you just want the money?
- Do you believe in love at first sight or shall I walk past you again?
- How do you like your eggs? Fertilized?
- Get your coat, love, you've pulled.
- Is that a ladder in your tights or the stairway to heaven?
- This body leaves in five minutes, be on it.
- Your clothes would look great on my bedroom floor.
- Can I have your picture so I can show Santa what I want for Christmas?
- I may not be the best-looking bloke in the room but I'm the only one talking to you.
- You're a thief: you've stolen my heart!
- Can I borrow your mobile? I told my parents I'd phone them when I met the girl of my dreams.
- Is it me or do you always look this good?
- The word 'beautiful' wouldn't be the same without U.

In 2004 Everards Brewery ran a competition which was won by the line: 'Well, here I am! What are your other two wishes?'

Meanwhile, in 2005, psychologists from Edinburgh and Lancashire universities addressed themselves to this vital subject. They didn't particularly rate direct requests for sex but thought these were better than the desperately corny: 'Do you have space in your bag for my BMW keys' and 'You're the star that completes the constellation of my existence'. Ouch!

According to Dr Christopher Bale, who led the research, 'The highest-rated lines were those reflecting the man's control of a situation, wealth, culture, and spontaneous wit.'

The scientists reckoned that examples of good lines were to say, 'Ten-ton polar bear,' and then, when you get a puzzled reply, retort, 'Well, it breaks the ice.' Another good idea is to steer the conversation towards music in order to say, 'The Moonlight Sonata or, to give it its true name, *Sonata quasi una fantasia*: a fittingly beautiful piece for a beautiful lady.' Sounds like the sort of thing you'd expect to hear from an Italian head waiter.

A better line was: 'There's something in your eye. Oh, it's a sparkle.'

The sad, prosaic truth is that if a bloke's good-looking enough then (almost) anything he says will work and, conversely, if he's an ugly bastard then (almost) anything he says won't work.

The same is true for women. Speaking strictly as a bloke, the line 'OK, all right then' works fine for me.

Is it true that royals are watched by flunkies while they have sex?

I phoned Buckingham Palace. No, honestly, I did. The first thing you hear is a taped voice saying, 'If you've been told to phone this number as a matter of urgency, then please hang up as it's a hoax' (or words to that effect). I got through to the press office and told an utterly charming woman that I was Mitchell Symons, the author of *Why Girls Can't Throw* – which prompted the usual five-minute conversation (useful as an ice-breaker). Then I asked my question – qualifying it as a real 'when did you stop beating your wife' question.

Lots of giggles.

'Never, surely!'

Well, obviously I knew that it wouldn't still be the case, but did it ever happen?

'You'd have to ask an historian.'

OK. But what about people having to witness royal births? Does that still happen?

She went away and came back a minute or so later. 'Princess Alexandra's birth in 1936 was the last occasion when a Home Secretary was required to be present.'

That's pretty recent.

She agreed, and went on to explain that until the reign of Queen Victoria, all sorts of lords, ladies and busybodies (my word, not hers) had to attend royal births – albeit in the room next door. Victoria cut it down to just one Cabinet minister – the Home Secretary – and so it continued until Christmas Day 1936 when Princess Alexandra was born.

King George VI then said that no one not directly in line to the throne would have to have their birth witnessed, and when, in 1948, a direct heir (Prince Charles) was born, King George VI decided that this arcane practice was 'neither a statutory requirement nor a constitutional necessity'.

As for the flunkies watching royals actually having sex, according to historian Dr Michael Morgan, 'not since medieval times and not always then. What tended to happen was that the newly married couple would be ceremoniously put to bed by their guests while the marriage bed would be blessed by a priest. Then the couple would consummate their marriage – usually unattended. They were expected to employ the missionary position – as it subsequently came to be known – because that was thought to be the only position to use to create boys. And boys were, of course, important for dynastic reasons.'

No one wears chastity belts any more ... *do they*?

I take it that you know what a chastity belt is? If not, I should explain that it's a locking appliance that prevents the wearer from engaging in sexual intercourse. In order to qualify as a chastity belt, it must be lockable.

These belts were first used in the Middle Ages to prevent women from being unfaithful and/or raped while their husbands were away at the Crusades.

So do they still exist? You bet!

There's a Sheffield company named Tollyboy ('Protecting your assets since 1956') which runs a thriving business on the internet selling female and male chastity belts/anti-rape devices, ankle, wrist and biceps bracelets and neck collars, as well as other products like plugs and restraints.

The company was founded by Hal Higginbottom, an engineer at Sheffield University who was challenged by a lecturer to make a modern-day chastity belt. When Higginbottom died in 1998, his apprentice, Richard Davies, took over the business and it was he who told me that 70 per cent of orders are from men.

To protect women or to stop them having fun?

'No, they are for men. Orders would run 70–75 per cent male belts, the female belt is a rarity. Belts are used as an aphrodisiac. Human nature being as it is, people want what they can't have.'

Was he satisfied that no one's actually being imprisoned in them?

'I know of no one who is imprisoned in one but that would be some people's fantasy. In any case, the police, fire brigade or any decent engineering firm could cut one off, so to keep someone imprisoned in one would require keeping them away from the outside world, phone or email etc.'

How much does a typical one cost and how many does he sell in a year?

'£300 and wildly variable but not enough to make much money.'

What do they call a Brazilian bikini wax in Brazil?

First of all, I should explain precisely what a 'Brazilian' is. It's a style of hair removal which leaves a woman with only the tiniest amount of pubic hair (other wise known as a 'landing strip'). The reason it's called a Brazilian is because the practice started in Brazil. During the 1990s, it was popularized in New York by Brazilian beauticians the J Sisters, whose salon apparently boasts an autographed photograph of Gwyneth Paltrow with the dedication: 'Thanks, you changed my life.'

• • • •

It's lucky for me that I lack the embarrassment gene because I have to tell you that even I found myself turning red as I phoned up all sorts of Brazilian organizations to ask them this incredibly daft question. True, most of them failed to understand what the hell I was talking about, but I think I managed to jeopardize Anglo-Brazilian relations for at least a generation.

Eventually, a very nice lady at somewhere called Brazilian Contemporary Arts agreed to help me. 'We just call it *depilar*,' she said, obviously marking me down as a true British eccentric or else yet another victim of the 'Care in the Community' programme.

Not a Colombian or a Peruvian or, indeed, a German?

'No, just *depilar*.'

But you're aware that the rest of the world calls it a Brazilian?

'Yes.'

And what do you think of that?

Silence.

Hello.

'Is that all you want?'

I suppose so. Thank you.

. . . .

I guess it was a dumb question but underlying it is something really rather important. What kind of society do we live in where women are told that shaving their pudenda to a little 'landing strip' – or indeed rendering them totally bald – is the fashionable thing to do?

And what kind of man finds a bald binky sexy? And why would any woman want to hook up with the sort of man who finds a bald binky sexy?

You take my point.

At this juncture, I should say that, when it comes to pubic hair, I really think a short back and sides (and shampoo) is all that any self-respecting woman should go in for. Do you remember the fashion designer Mary Quant, whose husband cut her pubic hair into a heart shape? Well, topiary's all very well, mate, but stick to hedges – not bushes.

Then there are the women who dye their pubic hair. Paula Yates (pink), Jayne Mansfield (blonde) and Carole Lombard (blonde) all did and none of them lived to see middle age – although unlike Jean Harlow (who dyed hers platinum blonde and actually died of peroxide poisoning as a result), there was admittedly no causation link.

Are the letters sent to 'men's' magazines genuine?

You know the sort of thing: 'Dear Sir, I always thought that the letters in your magazine were made up until I had an experience which I would like to share with your readers. I was travelling on this train when this fantastic-looking girl got on. To my delight, she sat directly opposite me. To my amazement, all the other passengers got off at the next stop. To my ...' Etc. etc.

As I've already mentioned, when it comes to men's magazines, I've got some form. Some 20 years ago, I used to contribute – no, not letters – articles to *Penthouse*. I – or rather my alter ego, Mike Hunter (try saying it a few times and you'll understand the choice of pseudonym) – wrote things like The *Penthouse* Guide To Hen Nights, The *Penthouse* Guide To Stag Nights, Love On The Dole and Convent Girls. The aim of the articles was to inform and entertain but never – as far as I was concerned – to arouse. I loved writing that sort of stuff and, indeed, I really do think that I did some of my best work for *Penthouse*. I never did find out whether the letters in that magazine were true or false. My guess is that they were based on readers' letters but were then embellished/cleaned up/tidied up as necessary.

So I phoned around some of the other guys I know who've worked for men's magazines and asked them for their opinion. The consensus was that almost all of the letters were indeed made up but that some were at least based on readers' true experiences. The chances are, though, that the readers' letters were likely to be the least interesting or, as one fellow – a veteran of jazz mags – put it, 'If they give you a boner, they're made up.'

Apart from anything, it's safer for the staff of gentlemen's magazines to write their own letters pages as it means that they won't be the victims of spoofs. One such magazine once found itself publishing a series of letters on the joys of sex with amputees. After a few months, it became obvious that the whole thing was a practical joke and, you might think fittingly, the magazine didn't have a leg to stand on.

'If they give you a boner, they're made up'

One in ten men? Surely not?

Does it even matter? As one gay friend put it when I asked him, 'I don't care what percentage of the male population is gay so long as the gay in my bed is 100 per cent!'

I think that it does because it's become such an emotive, totemic figure (and, no, I'm not talking about the one in ten that UB40 were singing about).

Bearing in mind the usual health warnings about statistics ('there are three types of lies: lies, damn lies and statistics'), this one would seem to have some kind of accuracy.

The one-in-ten goes back to Kinsey's original 1948 report. Since then, there have been many more investigations into the prevalence of homosexuality and the findings have been fairly consistent – if slightly lower.

10 per cent variously described themselves as homosexual, bisexual and 'something else'

In 1993, Janus & Janus found that 4 per cent of men considered themselves homosexual and 5 per cent bisexual – which adds up to 9 per cent. The equivalent figures for women were 2 and 3 per cent.

Much more recently, in 2005, Mosher, Chandra & Jones found that 90 per cent of men considered themselves to be heterosexual. Now that obviously leaves 10 per cent, or 'one in ten'. Unfortunately, it's a little more complicated than that because the other 10 per cent variously described themselves as homosexual, bisexual and 'something else'.

Interestingly, the figures were almost identical for women.

So what can we conclude?

I think we can safely say that 'one in ten' covers men who are not heterosexual. Beyond that, who can tell what people get up to in the privacy of their homes? Who can vouch for the accuracy and honesty of what respondents tell scientists and pollsters? Some men who are gay refuse to acknowledge it even to themselves.

There's an extra dimension too: during the writing of this book, I've learned just how fluid categories can be – and, therefore, how worthless categorization can be. What about the otherwise heterosexual man who has sexual thoughts about men? Or the o.h.m. who has anal sex with a post-operative transsexual woman? Or my friend (whose name I will not divulge – or at least not while he continues to pay me) who, although an o.h.m., likes nothing better than for his girlfriend to strap on a dildo and give him one up the bum?

And who knows where people go to when they're alone in their beds?

Do nuns and priests have to be virgins?

No, I'm not stupid: I know that nuns and priests are tied to their vows of chastity. What I wasn't so sure about, however, was whether a non-virgin was barred from the priesthood or from entering a convent.

So I phoned Father Paul Embury, director of the National Office for Vocation (the group responsible for the formation of priests).

'No,' said Father Paul, 'priests don't have to be virgins. When any candidate presents himself, we look at every facet of his life. We want to know his sexual history – not just physical sex. If somebody has been sexually active in the past, we'd want to see there'd been a period of abstinence and we'd want to know that they were orientating themselves towards a life of celibacy. Even someone who's in a relationship that's non-sexual, we'd want to know that they've put some distance between themselves and their girlfriend before they can commence with their formation and training.

'There's also a psychological assessment, which would take account of such issues.'

We've been talking about priests – do you happen to know if the same is true for nuns?

'Yes, it's the same.'

But then afterwards, of course, they have to be totally celibate.

'Yes, though interestingly, if a priest falls from grace, he's not automatically dismissed – although he would be expected to take responsibility for any child he fathered.

'There is also a slight difference between, on the one hand, monks and nuns and, on the other, priests. Monks and nuns take solemn vows of chastity, poverty and obedience, whereas diocesan priests take a promise of obedience and a promise of celibacy. Promises are not solemn vows. This is a nuance that not everyone would get. The difference being that a vow is binding whereas a promise isn't.'

Why wouldn't a priest make such a vow?

'Monks and nuns vow to remain celibate for the rest of their lives whereas, with priests, the Pope might change the stance on married priests, and then they wouldn't have to be celibate. And then there are the Anglican ministers who became priests after leaving their church over the ordination of women: they're not expected to be celibate.'

What is the greatest male sexual lie?

Well, for a start it might just be that you can't get pregnant if you have sex standing up (see page 99) – especially if uttered in order to persuade a girl to have unprotected sex.

Other than that, it's hard to know where to start – given that a man in possession of a stiffie is prepared to say pretty well almost anything for an invitation (note the juxtaposition of stiffie and invitation – rather clever, don't you think?).

Male sexual lies can be neatly divided into two distinct categories. Those told *before* sex (i.e. in pursuance of it) and those told *after* sex (i.e. to get away – bearing in mind the different male/female sexual imperatives discussed elsewhere).

BEFORE

- I'll still respect you in the morning.

- This is it.

- My partner and I have an open relationship.

- God, you're so beautiful.

- I won't tell a soul about this (used before with the stress on the fifth word; used after with the stress on the first word).

- I'll only put it in a little way.

- I never knew it could be like this.

- I want to wake up next to you in the morning.

- I promise I won't come in your mouth.

AFTER

- Of course I still respect you.

- I promise I won't tell anyone.

- There's no one else but you (also used before).

- You're really very attractive.

- I tried phoning you but you were constantly engaged.

- Thank God you phoned – I lost your telephone number.

What is the greatest female sexual lie?

When it comes to telling the truth before, during and after sex, women are, by far, the more honest gender. Or at least so they tell us and so we chaps like to think. But I suspect it's true because women are not only encouraged to be more in touch with their feelings but also to share them.

Having said that, they too are capable of mendacity. Here are some examples:

- **This is my very first one-night stand.**

- **My boyfriend and I are in the process of breaking up.**

- **You're the best.**

- **I've never done that with a man before.**

And which is the greatest female lie?

I think we all know that, fellows, don't we? Yup, that's right, it's: 'Of course I'll still do that when we're married.'

Why is the most common position for sexual intercourse called the missionary position?

On all things linguistic, I am obliged (through sheer indolence more than anything else) to consult Dr Karen Landy.

'Ah, you mean Venus Observa.'

Do I?

'That is its technical name.'

So why is it called the missionary position? Is it because it's what the missionaries told the natives was the 'proper' way to have sex?

'A common misconception, I'm afraid.'

Tee hee!

'What?'

Misconception. Good pun.

'If you say so,' she said glacially. 'In any event, the missionary position, in which the man lies on top of the woman, is a relatively recent expression dating from after World War Two.'

I was surprised. As recently as that?

'The expression, that is, not the position. Yes. It seems that missionaries didn't, in fact, express any opinion on how sex should be performed – why on earth would they? However, that didn't stop mischievous Pacific islanders from including them in their range of impersonations of how different people had sex.'

That's extraordinary!

'It is, isn't it? Of course the islanders themselves were more inclined to have sex with the woman on her hands and knees—'

Doggie style …

'Quite, and they decided to characterize the missionaries as being so strait-laced that they would only do it in – what the islanders considered to be – the least embarrassing fashion possible. From there, in what might be termed an intriguing self-fulfilling prophecy, the expression "missionary position" came to be the default description of the sexual position of a man lying on top of a woman.'

Are there any countries in which homosexuality is still illegal?

Yes.

Perhaps surprisingly, it's only been legal throughout the so-called enlightened West in the past few years – it was illegal in Ireland until 1993.

The countries where it's still illegal are, alas, the usual suspects: Muslim countries and African countries (though not South Africa).

As most people know, Sharia law forbids homosexuality, while in Africa, at the last count, male homosexuality was illegal in 29 countries and female homosexuality was illegal in 20.

It is also still illegal in India.

Premature ejaculation – doesn't it just save time?

Premature ejaculation is not uncommon. Google the two words and you get more than two million hits – many of them offering advice to sufferers.

So why is it shrouded in so much furtiveness? To give you an idea, these were the only famous p.e.rs I could find: King Edward VIII, John Maynard Keynes, Tony Curtis (in his youth), Havelock Ellis (until the age of 60 and without ever achieving vaginal penetration), Johann von Goethe (until his late 30s), Groucho Marx (all his life), Henry Fonda (according to ex-wife Margaret Sullavan), Rock Hudson (according to a woman he had sex with – now *he* probably did just want to save time) and John F. Kennedy (another man who would have wanted to save time – but only because he had so many more women to attend to).

Not a huge haul, is it? And that was after a truly epic trawl through all my extensive library.

As you'll soon know from the answer to the question Is It Possible For Men To Fake Orgasm? (page 134), I used to suffer from the opposite problem (no, not immature ejaculation) so I used to find it hard to sympathize or empathize much with chaps who were able to do it quicker than I could.

But after one member of my teenage crowd was 'outed' by a particularly cruel girl as a premature ejaculator, I realized that the inability to consummate a relationship for more than a few seconds could indeed be seen as an affliction.

Generations of Zen Buddhists have spent their lives contemplating the question 'Does the tree that falls in the forest make a sound if no one is there to hear it?' Me and my mates were a little more prosaic: 'Can a man be said to have had sex if the girl hasn't even noticed it?'

Cruel, I know, but this was the 1970s and we didn't know what consciousness was, let alone thought about raising it.

I never spoke to the poor lad about his problem. Indeed, as I recall, he sort of disappeared from the scene pretty soon afterwards.

The cruel girl married a residential estate agent. She deserved nothing better.

Canvassing my (current) friends, only one of them admitted to being a premature ejaculator – and, even then, only in his youth. Roger (for want of a better pseudonym) told me that, in his case, it was a mixture of nerves and lust. 'Just the thought that I was going to, you know, get it away was enough to set me off. Jeez, you spend all that time tugging away at yourself at the thought of having sex with a "real woman". Then, when the time comes, you explode as soon as you're about to start.'

I told him that I could understand that happening the first time – big build-up etc. – but surely not on subsequent occasions?

'Are you kidding? Those were even worse! Now the nerves started kicking in. You know, "Oh God, I hope I don't come too soon!" And of course you do: it's a self-fulfilling prophecy.'

How did you cure it?

He shrugged his middle-aged shoulders. 'Time heals most things. With enough repetition, you get less lustful and less nervous. Also Tina [his wife] helped enormously by not making a fuss of it when we were first together.'

Bet she wishes you were a little more premature these days.

There was a flash of youthful anger in his eyes. 'No, Mitch. To answer your original question: when it comes to sex, not all people want to "save time". Don't judge everyone's sex life by your own.'

Ouch.

What's so big (and clever) about bigamy?

What indeed?

Bigamy is one of those crimes that carries its own punishment – two wives and two mothers-in-law. Mind you, Oscar Wilde – not the most uxorious of men – reckoned, 'Bigamy is having one wife too many. Monogamy is the same.' Though to be fair to Oscar, I've also seen the same quote attributed to Erica Jong and Gloria Swanson – both of whom I have met, by the way (just thought I'd mention it).

Interestingly, there are very few instances of women committing bigamy. This isn't (just) because women are far too sensible to sign up for more than one husband – at least not concurrently – but because, generally speaking, women aren't as proficient as men at compartmentalization. This is the 'ability' to do or be something that would seem to conflict with another part of your life.

Bigamy has always been uncommon but it's particularly rare nowadays – partly because of better communications (especially mobile phones) and also because men don't have to marry women just to get a leg over so there's less incentive.

Indeed, in my researches, I found very few 'famous' bigamists. Rudolph Valentino, George Gissing, Jerry Lee Lewis (at age 16!), Anaïs Nin, Judy Garland and Steven Seagal were all wittingly or unwittingly married to two people simultaneously. It is also said that John F. Kennedy married a socialite named Durie Malcom in 1939 and was still married to her in 1953 when he married Jacqueline Bouvier. Meanwhile, Dame Cleo Laine (mother), Sir Michael Redgrave (father), Patrick Mower (father) and Lord Jeffrey Archer (father) all had bigamous parents.

Why do men (especially men in pubs) assume that the more desirable a woman is, the more she'll desire them?

You know what I mean. A group of guys are gathered together in a pub. A beautiful woman walks in and the conversation goes something like this:

> **''king hell! Did you see that?'**
> 'Phwoar!'
> **'Ooh, get your gums round those!'**
> 'She's gorgeous!'
> **'Bet she loves it!'**
> 'Not many!'
> **'She's mad for it!'**
> 'Dirty cow!'

All right, so the dialogue owes more than a little to *The Sweeney* but you get the drift. The woman has done nothing more provocative than walk into a public house in possession of a beautiful face.

So what's it all about?

I decided to consult the eminent psychiatrist Anne Kreeger.

'What do you think it's all about?'

I'm sorry, I came here for answers, not questions.

'Think about it, Mitch,' she said, crossing and uncrossing her (really rather nice) legs in a way that reminded me of Dr Jennifer Melfi in *The Sopranos*.

I don't know, maybe she gives off some sort of signal; maybe her beauty is predicated on that.

'No!' She made me feel like a particularly stupid student. She saw my face fall. 'Well, perhaps, but no, that's not it. They're projecting their desires on to her. This is something that men, particularly, are wont to do. The men find this woman beautiful and sexy and so they choose to believe that she's "gagging for it".'

Psychological term is that, Doc?

'What?'

Gagging for it.

'You'd be surprised the language we use when we're not working. But it's interesting that you contextualize this encounter with a group in a pub – thereby adding the two key factors of peer group pressure and inebriation to the situation.'

Do celibates get more work done than the rest of us?

I see no more action than any other happily married middle-aged man, but by no stretch of the imagination could I be described as a celibate.

And it's not only the (limited) time I spend in blissful sexual congress that I'm obliged to consider but also the (not so limited) time I spend thinking about sex. All right, so I also get to work, eat, watch sport on TV and play internet poker – none of which involve sex (except, at the moment, writing this book) – but it's rare that my libido is disengaged for long.

That's how it goes.

I have an acquaintance who once mentioned to me that he and his partner didn't go in for sex any more.

So I phoned him and told him I was writing a book and could he help me with this question. And guess what? He demanded anonymity! I can't think why …

Anyway, Vivien, as I shall call him, confirmed that he is (effectively) celibate. 'I have such a low sex drive – always have had – that it seemed easier to desist altogether rather than leaving it up in the air.'

What about your partner?

'She's fine with it. Truth be told, she was never much up for it in the first place. Sex was never important to our relationship – except in the breach: that's to say, at different times, we each felt guilty for not doing more about it. The day we decided simply to stop having sex was the best day in our relationship.'

So do you get more work done than non-celibates?

He chuckled. 'I do, but it's not quite for the reason that you think. Look, let's say that the average guy of our age has sex once a week and that that lasts for, say, 20 minutes.'

OK, but that would include the foreplay and the obligatory cuddle afterwards.

'Of course! But seriously, Mitch, 20 minutes is nothing out of a week containing several thousand minutes. How much more work would you be able to do in that time – always assuming that you would do any work at eleven o'clock on a Saturday night? No, the big difference between me and you isn't that you have sex and I don't, it's that you think about it and I don't. *That's* where I save time. I don't fuck secretaries—'

Nor do I!

'I don't have affairs—'

Nor do I!

'I'm not led around by my dick ...'

Ah, you've got me there.

'So all that time you spend thinking about it, talking about it, wondering about it, worrying that you're not getting as much as you think you ought to be, looking it up on the internet – that's all time you could be working. So yes, on that basis, I'd say that celibates do get more work done than sad sacks like you.'

I am NOT a sad sack. Am I?

Or is to ask the question to answer it?

Oh dear.

And the three famous celibates who spring to mind would all seem to support my friend's contention: Sir Cliff Richard (the guy's prolific, prodigious output could never have been achieved if he'd been having his nuts emptied on a regular basis), Ann Widdecombe (surprisingly not unattractive as I discovered when I found myself debating euthanasia alongside her at the Oxford Union but whose full curriculum vitae speaks volumes for a life without nookie) and Sir Alfred Hitchcock, who was celibate from the age of 42 and went on to direct some of his greatest films thereafter.

How devoted to watersports do you have to be to do it after eating asparagus?

In *Why Girls Can't Throw*, I tried to answer the question of why it was that asparagus makes our wee-wee smell (turns out that it doesn't affect everyone but for those of us who have this gene, there's a sulphurous compound found in foods like asparagus and garlic which, when broken down by our digestive systems, comes out in our urine half an hour later. And it smells rank).

Anyway, the point I'm making is that although I am prepared to accept that there are people who enjoy peeing on each other – it's not called watersports for nothing – might there not be a limit to aficionados' enthusiasm?

It was time to call my mate Rick.

'Oh yes,' he said cheerily enough, 'I'm definitely on for watersports. Though not for hardsports ... '

Hardsports? That's a new one on me?

'Poo-poos.'

Oh no, that's disgusting!

'Why? If that's what consenting adults – even Liberal Democrat MPs – want to do?'

Because ... because ...

'You are so judgemental! I don't do hardsports because it doesn't appeal but if it did or if I were with a woman who really really wanted me to—'

Enough! Go back to watersports!

'All right. Having a really sexy girl pissing all over you in a golden shower can be just fabulous ...'

I'll take your word for it.

'Yes, you will, won't you? And if she wants me to do it to her, why not? It's only water, after all.'

Aha, but what if one of you has been eating asparagus?

'I hear what you're saying but in the moment – I mean, at the precise moment in time that you're doing it, you just don't care. It simply doesn't matter. That's the whole point of great sex, you suspend your normal fastidiousness and just go for it. Except, of course, *you* don't, do you?'

I thanked him for his contribution and reflected on what he'd said. And you know what? I hear what *he's* saying and I know I'm old-fashioned, but there are some things that really are a step too far and piss smelling of asparagus is one of 'em.

Why do women on HRT always look as if they've just emerged from a tanning parlour?

I am aware that many of the questions in this book are not necessarily on the tip of every tongue. This, for example, is obviously quite a recherché question (if recherché means what I think it means). Chances are you've never even stopped to think about such a question – let alone lain awake at night pondering it. But grant me this at least, whenever a female celebrity of a certain age appears in a magazine or goes on TV to extol the virtues of Hormone Replacement Therapy, she does seem to have the most extraordinary suntan. In fact, I'd go so far as to say that they're almost orange.

Why?

Is there a link or is it just coincidence? Or am I plain wrong?

I wouldn't even begin to know how to answer such a question but Mrs Symons, a fine woman as I think I've already told you, is approaching the sort of age when she might just benefit from a little knowledge on the subject, so I asked her to report from the front line.

She accepted the assignment and, more to the point, accepted the premise behind the question.

After an exhaustive study – which, for some reason, seemed to necessitate an awful lot of expensive girlie lunches – she told me that there is a sort of cause and effect but that it's more cosmetic than medical.

'Before a woman goes on HRT, she's usually feeling pretty rundown. That's why she takes it.'

Sounds fair enough.

'Once she takes HRT – and don't you just hate people who pronounce the letter "H" as "haitch" instead of "aitch" – she will often feel an enormous improvement in her general sense of well-being and in her sex life.'

Why would that make her skin change colour?

'Wait for it, I'm getting there. Feeling good about herself makes her want to feel even better about herself. Suddenly, she's taking additional pride in her appearance. Hence the tan – real or fake. She wants to look her best.'

Even at the risk of turning orange?

'Even at the risk of turning orange. By the way, you should know that this is a huge industry. Statistics show that between 20 and 50 per cent of women in the Western world who are between the ages of 45 and 70 have taken or are now taking HRT.'

How does it work?

'HRT controls hot flushes and night sweats and relieves vaginal soreness due to dryness. It also reduces hip fractures caused by osteoporosis or "crumbling bones".'

OK. And it doesn't make you turn orange?

'Not necessarily.'

Suddenly, I needed reassurance. '*You're* not going to turn orange, are you?'

But answer came there none, and I now live in almost perpetual dread that one day I will end up with a missus who's half woman/half Jaffa.

Is it possible to die of a broken heart?

The answer to this question illustrates a wider point about mankind: our eagerness to distance ourselves from our emotions.

Let me explain. Hundreds of years ago, grief was accepted as a perfectly valid cause of death. Then 'reason' and 'enlightenment' taught us to treat such a proposition with scorn, and it is only recently that the medical establishment has looked at cases of sudden cardiac arrest precipitated by strong emotional distress and concluded that it is indeed possible to die of a broken heart.

Tell that to Johnny Cash – except you can't because he died of a broken heart just four months after the death of his wife, June.

Just like the former prime minister James Callaghan, who died 11 days after the death of his beloved wife, Audrey.

However, notwithstanding these two cases, the type of heart attack we're talking about – when an otherwise healthy person suffers from such intense stress that they die (the technical name for it is 'stress cardiomyopathy') – is much more common for women than it is for men.

The reason for this could be prosaic: namely, that men are more likely to die before their wives and therefore there are more broken-hearted women than there are men. Though, having said that, it should be pointed out that it is not only death that can precipitate the deadly release of the stress hormones that can stun the heart, but also traumatic break-ups and shocks. So perhaps we have to think again why women are so much more likely to be affected. Scientists have been reduced to surmising that it might have 'something to do with their hormones' or the way in which 'their brains are wired to their hearts'. In other words, who can say?

A study was conducted by the Johns Hopkins School of Medicine, which looked at 19 patients (all but one women) who had had what at first seemed to be traditional heart attacks, between 1999 and 2003. All the patients had experienced sudden emotional stress (news of a death, being present during an armed robbery, involvement in a car accident, even finding themselves at their own surprise party). The important thing was that although most were quite elderly, none had a history of heart problems.

When these people were compared with people who had had more 'conventional' heart attacks, they found that the 19 patients' arteries were healthy and unclogged but that the levels of stress hormones (such as adrenaline) in their blood were two to three times as high as in the 'conventional' heart-attack victims and seven or more times higher than normal.

According to Dr Wittstein of Johns Hopkins: 'Our hypothesis is that massive amounts of these stress hormones can go right to the heart and produce a stunning of the heart muscle that causes this temporary dysfunction resembling a heart attack. It doesn't kill the heart muscle like a typical heart attack, but it renders it helpless.'

Although people can – and do – make a full recovery from stress cardiomyopathy, there is obviously a serious problem with those victims whose original attack was precipitated by the loss of a loved one (as opposed to a shock) because although they might recover physically, there is less incentive for them to do so.

Do bisexuals, *pace* Woody Allen, have double the chance of a date on a Saturday night?

'Bloody greedy bastards,' said my mate Pete, the saloon bar sexologist, somewhat surprisingly. 'They want to make up their minds which side they're on.'

Are you kidding?

'All right, you got me – but I do feel a teensy bit pissed off with fellows who bat for both sides.'

Why?

'Look, if they go with other men, they're gay, right? Nothing wrong with that: leaves more for the rest of us. But if they also play for our side, then they're using up valuable resources.'

I pointed out that he seemed to have no problem with female bisexuals.

'On the contrary, the more the merrier: there's nothing I like better than a pair of carpet-munchers getting it on.'

It's only when I'm with Neanderthals like Pete that I realize just how high my consciousness has been raised over the years.

'People just used to have sex with whoever – or indeed, WHATEVER – was at hand.'

Fortunately, I also have access to intelligent people – like the social anthropologist Dr Lorraine Mackintosh.

'You must remember,' she said, 'that it's only in (relatively) recent times that we've categorized people at all. People just used to have sex with whoever – or, indeed, *whatever* – was at hand. Homosexuality, per se, is very much a 19th-century construct.

'Obviously, heterosexual sex has always been necessary for the continuation of the species, but when it comes to recreational sex, there

95

have been ages that are less strait-laced than ours.'

I'm surprised by that. I've always thought that mankind has become more permissive as it's evolved.

'Some and some. Social mores never follow a simple straight trajectory. And behaviour can be extremely widespread and yet not be officially sanctioned by the society that, effectively, nurtures it.'

All very helpful but it was time for me to find myself a living, breathing bisexual.

This wasn't as easy as it sounds. I know plenty of gays and lesbians but not – or so I assumed – any bisexuals.

In fact, it was only when I was asking my friend Hugh – whom I'd always taken to be exclusively gay – for help with finding someone who swings both ways that he revealed that he himself fits that bill.

'I didn't know that,' I said, almost indignantly.

'There are lots of things you don't know about me. You know, Mitch, if you have a defect, it's that you tend to put people into boxes. Gay, straight, married, single. Life's more fluid than that. Sometimes, it's more complicated; sometimes it's simpler. To quote the late James Dean, "Why should I go through life with one hand tied behind my back?"'

Hang on, I spluttered, I've never seen you with a woman.

'Oh, I see, just because you don't know something, it doesn't happen. Does the tree that falls in the forest make a sound if—'

Don't get me started …

'No, the point I'm making is that it *does* make a sound – yeah, even if Mitchell Symons doesn't happen to

'Why should i go through life with one hand tied behind my back?'

witness it. So, yes, I'm a gay man but if I fancy a woman – and she fancies me – then I've no problem obliging myself. And her.'

All right then, does being a bisexual double your chances … ?

'I'm not a "bisexual". Stop putting me in categories! I'm me – Hugh. Sometimes – usually – I have sex with men, and sometimes I have sex with women. And if I want to have sex with an animal, I would do that too. But that wouldn't make me a "bestialist". Any more than playing tennis once a month makes me a tennis player.'

I didn't know you played tennis.

'The list of things you don't know is—'

I get it. Well, does being a bisexual – I mean, does being prepared to sleep with anyone … I mean, you know what I mean …

He put me out of my misery. 'I very rarely spend an evening alone – except out of choice. But that's not because I'm gay, straight or bisexual but because I am totally gorgeous.'

If you say so, Hugh.

Do men *really* think about sex every six seconds?

As seldom as that, eh?

No, I'm only kidding – though when it comes to matters of sex, I do have a tendency to revert to my teenage self. But even then, I doubt if I thought about 'it' more often than, ooh, twice an hour – tops. There are other things in life, you know. Why else did God invent food, sport and television?

Precisely.

So where does this 'six seconds' idea come from?

Incredibly, nobody knows.

So, almost by default, we can conclude that it's a generic put-down by women – a line like 'men are so pathetic, they think about sex all the time' evolves into 'men are so pathetic, they think about sex all the time – every ten seconds, I've heard'. Being more specific is a classic way of spreading a mistruth (see Marianne Faithfull and the Mars Bar – there was, as I explained in *Why Girls Can't Throw,* no confectionery in the Mick & Keef drugs bust but that didn't stop people saying that there was and then 'proving' it by specifying the product). From ten seconds to six seconds is then simply a matter of embellishment.

For what it's worth, according to the Kinsey Institute, 54 per cent of men think about sex every day or several times a day, 43 per cent a few times per month or a few times per week, and 4 per cent less than once a month. By comparison, 19 per cent of women think about sex every day or several times a day, 67 per cent a few times per month or a few times per week, and 14 per cent less than once a month.

Six seconds indeed!

And how much time would that leave for internet poker?

Can you get pregnant if you have sex standing up?

At my MPSIA (Minor Public School I'm Afraid), we were offered a choice between studying Latin and Biology. I chose the former and thus I know absolutely NOTHING about the human body and how it works. Oh, sure I know that we have 206 bones and that the smallest one is in the ear but that comes under the heading of trivia rather than anything more useful.

In fact, so ignorant am I on the subject that I used to believe – until not that long ago – that the gender of a baby was determined by which of the two participants in the act of procreation had tried harder. Honestly.

As I write these words, I'm aware of a lack of knowledge that's almost scary in its implications. I mean, are you familiar with something called 'tyrannical ignorance'? It's where you don't know what it is you don't know. In other words, you not only don't know the answer, you don't even know the question to ask.

With so many of the questions in this book, I find myself beset with tyrannical ignorance – and no more so than here.

How does the woman's reproductive system work? Are there bits inside women that might make a difference to the answer? Who knows? My knowledge of the female form is almost entirely derived from smutty magazines. I feel disorientated when I see a naked woman without staples in her midriff.

Now for the question. By the way, this is what's known in the journalism biz as a dropped intro. Just thought you'd like to know (you can't say you don't learn things here). I always half-believed that having sex standing up was as inconsequential as eating standing up but that's obviously a case of the wish being father to the thought. So let's take two couples: Couple 1 and Couple 2. Couple 1 always have sex standing up; Couple 2 always do it lying down. Surely Couple 1 would be less likely to conceive (always assuming that everything was equally OK with both couples' plumbing)?

I decided to phone the British Pregnancy Advisory Service whose spokeswoman, Vishnee Sauntoo, is doubly qualified as she's also a biotechnologist. 'No, I'm certain that it makes no difference. I used to work for the Human Fertilization and Embryology Authority – the IVF watchdog – so putting that hat on I would say that it wouldn't make any difference.'

With more patience – and kindness – than I deserved, she went on to explain that it was definitely possible to get pregnant if you have sex standing up.

At this point, we had an 'aha moment', as Vishnee said that the more stressed you were, the less likely you were to conceive.

Hang on, I said, does this mean that the couple who didn't care about conception were more likely to conceive than—

She finished off my sentence: ' ... than the couple who were undergoing IVF treatment and experiencing all the stress that goes with it.'

Which explains why supposedly infertile couples can't have children until they adopt and then – hey presto – the woman gets pregnant.

Before letting Vishnee go, I asked her to confirm or deny the theory that having sex in a certain position can help determine the gender of a baby but her response was, 'We're not aware of that.'

Where's the most extraordinary place anyone's ever had sex?

This question reminds me of a wonderful (hopefully true) story. They were doing a roadshow of the popular TV game show *Mr & Mrs*. The presenter (not the show's then TV host, Derek Batey) asked a man, 'Where's the most unusual place you've had sex?' After some prompting, the man admitted that he and his wife had 'done it' in a golf bunker on their honeymoon. His wife was then brought into the room and asked the same question. She looked to her husband for reassurance. He told her to go ahead. 'Up me bum,' was her reply.

No, I think we're talking about physical rather than human geography. My claim to infamy is that I once did it with an obliging girlfriend between Golders Green and Hampstead tube stations on the Northern Line of the London Underground (I should say that the carriage was totally empty and it is one of the longest stops on the system). But you don't want to hear about my experiences, you want to know about celebrities, so let me see what I can find.

James Boswell – Dr Johnson's amanuensis – did it on Westminster Bridge with a prostitute (which made a nice change from his usual habitat of St James's Park).

Clark Gable and **Carole Lombard** did it in a duck blind (a shelter for concealing duck hunters).

Lynne Perrie did it 'on top of Table Mountain in Cape Town'.

However, the award for the most inventive tryst must go to the late Brian Glover, who once consummated his passion 'in the British Museum'. Top man.

Why don't men blow?

OK, so this is a riff on the title question of the previous book, *Why Girls Can't Throw* (they can, they can), but there is a serious question to be answered.

Why are men so reluctant to perform cunnilingus? Is it disinterest in a woman's pleasure (for the many women who find it pleasurable)? Is it just squeamishness?

Or is it – and I'm sorry but there's no other way I can put this – the smell?

Specifically, the smell of fish.

Look, I'm not trying to gross you out but there is a problem out there (or, rather, down there).

So what causes this smell? Incredibly, according to my researches, it's smegma. Yup, the same stuff that makes blokes' pricks honk is also responsible for fishy fannies. Whaddya know? It isn't unique to men. Apparently, the same stuff gathers under the clitoris hood where, if it's not washed away regularly, it develops into a powerful sexual deterrent.

But why smegma? What is it? Is there any point to it?

Incredibly, there is. For men, it moisturizes the glans to keep it soft and smooth: for women, it performs the same function for the clitoris. For both genders, smegma has beneficial antibacterial and antiviral properties which keep all our nether regions healthy.

But is it a fishy smell or am I merely universalizing my own reaction?

I decided to consult my frontiersman friend, Rob (the guy who answered the questions Why Don't We Eat Squirrels? and Why Is It Easier To Park A Car Backwards Than Forwards? in *WGCT*). Rob is a man of many answers, but he also has a special expertise when it comes to answering this question. No, not (as he would like us to believe) because he's a fine and sensitive lover of huge experience but because he's totally allergic to ALL fish. Just the merest taste of tuna will cause him to upchuck everywhere. I haven't actually seen him do his projectile-vomiting stuff but he assures me that it is a memorable sight.

Anyway, given that Rob is so allergic to fish, is he also allergic to whiffy pussies?

'Yes, sometimes.'

So there you have it. Proof, if proof were needed, that the smell of unwashed binky is, indeed, piscine (it means 'relating to fish', not 'relating to French swimming pool)'.

Anyway, I trust that explains why some men are reluctant to blow some women. It's for precisely the same reason that some women are reluctant to blow some men: lousy hygiene. There's no point in men and women taking the trouble to dress up for each other if they're not going to wash themselves first. The neglect of intimate parts will, necessarily, militate against intimacy.

It's interesting to note that our fathers' generation had to be persuaded to use underarm deodorant. Thankfully, BO is now a rarity, and perhaps it's time to address ourselves to our nether regions with the same zeal. Although, I should stress that, except in extreme cases, I am opposed to the use of 'hygiene products': soap and water will do nicely.

All right, so that's disposed of one important reason why men don't blow – what about the others?

I consulted a few of my (male) friends and their answers were all pretty similar, which is, I guess, a function of being middle-aged, married and a friend of mine.

None of them are – or, at least, none of them admitted to being – keen carpet-munchers.

Why? 'Because,' said one who demanded anonymity, 'it's about my pleasure, not hers.'

Another friend told me it was reserved for 'high days and holidays and, if truth be told, we both keep score of who did it last'.

'The only smell here is the whiff of misogyny'

Yet another reckoned, 'It's not worth the effort – besides, she never goes down on me.'

So there you have it: it's a combination of selfishness and laziness.

I think there might be a bit more to many men's disinclination to perform oral sex (though not, you can be sure, when it comes to receiving it). There's also the male psyche to consider: it's about cutting to the chase, getting to the destination. Any foreplay merely delays the main event and, for many men, is more a necessary chore than a pleasure to be enjoyed for its own sake. After men have achieved their own orgasms, they could start cunnilingusing then, but for so many men – yes, including this one if I'm honest – once we've come, it's game over.

Obviously I had absolutely no intention of discussing any of this with a real live woman, but unfortunately such a person got to read it and was extremely indignant.

'The only smell here is the whiff of misogyny,' she declared.

Eh?

'I've never known a man who didn't like giving head. It's highly arousing for both parties. You're just an old fogey.'

I'm only three years older than you.

'Yeah, but somehow we manage to belong to different generations. Every generation thinks they invented sex, but my generation, who became teenagers in the mid-1970s, believe we invented oral sex, and now, thanks to you, I know that's true.'

Oops.

'I suppose it's possible that in a case of extremely poor hygiene, or even poor health, a woman would give off a smell and that that smell might be characterized by fishiness. But it's by no means a regular state of affairs. The natural lubricant doesn't smell unless it's been allowed to get stale. OK, look, on the hygiene front I might concede one thing. That's the fixed-head shower.'

What?

'A girl can't have a decent wash under a fixed-head shower. If you're not going to have a bath, then you need a detachable shower head. You've got to get that thing off the wall and play it on the right spot. Which, might I add, is not at all a bad way to start the day.'

If you say so.

Is sex a good form of exercise?

A really intensive session is more beneficial than a gym workout (and a lot more fun) and even married sex is better than no sex at all – I'm sorry, I meant 'no exercise at all'.

For example, for the average person, 15 minutes of 'average' (you know what I mean) sex – with five minutes of foreplay – uses up about 100 calories.

Not shabby.

And to that you can add the calories used up undressing each other. According to a professor from Italy – where else? – undoing a bra with two hands uses up eight calories while undoing it with just one hand uses up a whopping 18 calories.

And then there's the French kissing, which expends up to six calories per minute – so a ten-minute full and frank exchange of tongues would make up for – ooh – at least a finger of KitKat.

And that's without including the number of calories burned in chasing after/nagging your partner for sex.

But even if they refuse to play, the lack of a partner is no bar to losing weight through sex: according to something called the Young People's Reproductive and Sexual Health & Rights Organization, an act of masturbation burns up between 100 and 150 calories.

This leads me to conclude that I'm not overweight because I eat too much but because I wank too little. This is easily remedied.

What are the benefits (if any) of swallowing?

Loads.

Huge benefits – no question about it. In fact, the following message appeared in my email box just the other day.

>> Women who perform the act of fellatio on a regular basis, one to two times a week, may reduce their risk of breast cancer by up to 40 per cent, a recent study found. Doctors had never suspected a link between the act of fellatio and breast cancer, but new research being performed is starting to suggest that there could be an important link between the two.

In a study of over 15,000 women suspected of having performed regular fellatio over the past ten years, the researchers found that those actually having performed the act regularly, one to two times a week, had a lower occurrence of breast cancer than those who had not. There was no increased risk, however, for those who did not regularly perform.

It was, of course (and alas), a joke.

And I hope that those women who fell for it took it in the spirit it was intended.

Yeah, right.

But are there any benefits?

Before I go any further, do you know the difference between love, true love and showing off? The answer is, respectively, spitting, swallowing and gargling.

But are there any benefits?

It's probably no better – or worse – than the average beverage. Let's say that the average emission is 10cc (yup, that's how they got their name) and it's nine-tenths water, which has no calories. So we're talking about 1cc of mainly sugar (fructose to be precise), a little fat and a tiny bit of protein.

But are there any benefits?

Well, it won't cure cancer – or even a cold – but think how pathetically grateful the recipient would be and then you tell me what the benefits are.

So, all those initials, what do they stand for?

We're talking about the sorts of initials found on the sorts of sites that the sorts of chaps who put together this sort of books are obliged to visit. Sites where 'working girls' ply their trade.

Some of them – like 'A', 'O' and 'BJ' (respectively 'Anal', 'Oral' and 'Blow Job') – are obvious, but others are positively mystifying. So, in the interests of elucidation, here are some of the more common (*le mot juste*) acronyms.

AWO: Anal WithOut (without, that is, a condom: in other words, total lunacy for both parties. See also BBBF).

BBBF: BareBack Butt Fuck (bareback means without a condom. See also AWO).

BBBJ: BareBack Blow Job (see also OWO).

BBF: BareBack Fuck (again not advised unless you like playing Russian roulette with your immune system. See also SWO).

BBW: Big Beautiful Woman (fat and/or big-breasted. Judging by some of the photos I've seen, the second 'b' is frequently misleading. If they want alliteration, what's wrong with 'blubbery', 'bovine' or 'bleedin' ugly').

BDSM: Bondage, Domination (or Discipline), Submission (or Sadism), Masochism (and all that sort of thing).

CIM: Come In Mouth (facility offered at the end of a BBBJ. Sometimes followed by the words 'and swallow'. Not the sort of thing you get at home).

CP: Corporal Punishment (or the Conservative Party which, in the good old days, was one and the same thing).

CWM: Cyber WhoreMonger (a punter who uses the internet. Not to be confused with the Welsh word 'cwm' meaning 'village'. Nor indeed with the Council for World Mission, which is a Christian charity organization).

DP: Double Penetration (two men, one woman – you get the picture. More often used in pornography than in prostitution).

GFE: GirlFriend Experience.

OTK: Over The Knee (spanking. Also known as the English Disease – but not in England).

OWO: Oral WithOut (see also BBBJ).

SWO: Sex WithOut (see also BBF).

WS: Water Sports (but rarely performed with water. In the interests of accuracy – and to pre-empt embarrassing confusion at the beach – should perhaps be renamed 'Wee-wee Sports').

Is it really inadvisable for a sportsman to have sex before a match?

My idea of a sporting contest being a light game of pool at my local, I'm hardly the man to answer this question.

It's true that in my rugby-playing days (Old Millhillians Extra Bs), I would occasionally strike it lucky on a Friday night without it noticeably affecting my performance on a Saturday afternoon, but I was always such a lacklustre player that how could anyone have told?

So I phoned Dr Roland Powell, my pet MD, and he told me that the jury was out on this one. 'Some people abstain because they think it focuses their mind on the following day's contest whereas others believe that the release of tension through sex helps them. Some experts believe the presence of testosterone in the body can be advantageous to sportsmen in power sports – like weightlifting or sprinting – but whether this is better achieved by activity or abstinence is a matter of debate.'

I did some investigating into specific cases but couldn't arrive at any definite conclusion.

In 2005 Sven Goran Eriksson banned the England team from having sex before a big game. Mind you, the year before a 'busty glamour girl' told the *People* that she and an England player had had sex before a match with no apparent adverse effects. The player was also unaffected.

Another top sportsman to be grassed up to a red-top tabloid was a tennis player. A French 'model' told the *News of The World* that the player 'always said good sex before a match was worth a few points each set. He loved having sex just before he was due on court – even at Wimbledon.'

On the other hand, the Arsenal and Swedish footballer Freddie Ljungberg once admitted, 'After having sex the night before, I lose all feelings in my feet.' (Boy, is he doing something wild …)

Having said that, the Brazilian Ronaldo sometimes scores before a match and he's been quoted as saying, 'It helps me to play better too,' while the great Rod Stewart, who is still playing soccer in his seventh decade, usually has sex before a game (and, who knows, given the man's legendary libido, maybe at half-time too).

When Steve Davis found himself falling down the snooker (now *there's* a sport) rankings, he tried everything to improve his performance – including sexual abstinence before a game (but it wasn't that that inspired his remarkable career renaissance in 2006).

My conclusion is that much of it is in the mind – either way – and that so long as a sportsman is in the right mental state (however he achieves that), then he'll perform to his full potential.

Are any foods really aphrodisiacs?

You won't be surprised to learn that I belong to the school of thought that says if you're in the mood then almost nothing will stop you, and that if you're not, then almost nothing will work (except maybe Rohypnol).

Still, in the interests of scientific research, I unearthed the following so-called aphrodisiacs.

Oysters These are high in calcium, iron and vitamin A – all of which help with the process of 'lurve'. In fact, *all* shellfish – especially lobster – have aphrodisiacal qualities. The truth is that if you're taken (or you're taking someone) out for a lobster supper, you're going to be pretty turned on anyway.

Sunflower seeds Apparently, these have to be 'raw'. Is there any other way?

Cabbage Now, I like cabbage – especially with roast beef – but I was as amazed to learn about its supposedly invigorating effect on libido as I was to learn about carrots and turnips, which are apparently also aphrodisiacs. Though in the case of turnips, it's only the tops that are of use.

Tomatoes You always knew that salad was good for you – well, now you can order double portions. And tomato isn't the only thing that will pep up your love life. While you're at it (or, indeed, *before*, if you catch my drift), check out some avocado, cucumber, green pepper, watercress and lettuce.

Lemon Maybe this explains why cocktail bars always give you a slice of lemon with your drink: they're trying to get you in the mood. In fact, all citrus fruit is good to eat if you want a healthy sex life.

Honey This contains something called the 'gonadotropic hormone', which apparently helps to stimulate the sex glands.

Garlic Now this poses an interesting dilemma: you eat garlic to make yourself sexier but, of course, the more you eat, the less fanciable you become. Hmm. The same problem also applies to that other supposed aphrodisiac, onions.

Radishes This raises similar problems to garlic and onions, and also the possibility of wind, which is, let's face it, hardly the greatest turn-on.

Betel nut (if you chew it). If you remember *South Pacific*, you'll remember Bloody Mary, the brothel madam, 'chewing betel nut'.

Strawberries Tastier than many of the above 'remedies', strawberries will apparently put you in the mood for almost anything.

And so the list goes on – culminating in, of course, chocolate, which, according to all the women I've consulted, isn't just an aphrodisiac for sex but a damn fine alternative to it too. Not surprising when you consider that it contains trace amounts of phenylethylamine, the same chemical found in the brains of people who are in love.

Then there are all the weird things – like snake blood and powdered rhino horn – but, frankly, it's not worth the bother, is it?

The truth is, for most humans of my gender, almost anything will do – including the word 'the', as Derek and Clive (aka Peter Cook and Dudley Moore) demonstrated in *Ad Nauseam* (1978).

Is fidelity no big deal for gay couples?

I ask this question because many of the gay men I have known have been (not to put too fine a point on it) utter slags. One old friend in particular used to come into my office at the BBC in the morning just to tell me how many men he'd had sex with the night before on Hampstead Heath.

I asked him why he was so promiscuous and he told me that of the two things, coming out as gay and being promiscuous, the former had been far more of a stigma than the latter could ever be.

Mind you, that was some 25 years ago and he had been married with children at the point when he came out.

What about today's gays?

Another gay friend explained gay promiscuity thus: 'With a man and a woman, you have – or at least traditionally you had – the woman saying, "No, we shouldn't!" With gays, you have two men both saying, "Yeah!"'

In other words, it's the irresistible force meeting the *moveable* object.

So does this explain gay infidelity?

Once again, I turned – alas, for him, only metaphorically – to Simon Fanshawe. First of all, he invited me to consider all the gay relationships where fidelity *is* a big deal. He is, of course, absolutely right: I can think of at least three gay couples I know who have been together for years and are the model of fidelity. And then there are all the civil partnerships that have sprung up in the wake of the new law (in 2006).

Still, did Simon know what I was driving at?

'Yes, I do. Relationships in the absence of children have a different dynamic. In relationships with children, there is a kind of construct, a template that they're playing out. Where there are no children, you make different kinds of choices.'

So he doesn't distinguish between gay and straight but between couples with and without children. It makes sense to me.

'I know many people who are each other's life partners. However, they might have one-off casual relationships or more serious relationships that are still clearly secondary to their principal relationship. It was different in the past. There was a time when gay men saw themselves as endlessly promiscuous and lived their lives accordingly.'

Like children who have suddenly been given the keys to the sweet shop?

'Absolutely! A blade of grass was privacy enough for us. Now we've become a much more accepted part of wider society, we find ourselves behaving in the way that other straight members of that society behave. In other words, once you lay a place at the table, you eat differently with other people than you did when you were eating on your own in the kitchen.'

it's the irresistible force meeting the *moveable* object

What's the most exotic love offering ever made?

You know that bunch of roses (three for a fiver) you bought off that bloke on the central reservation of the A3 last Valentine's Day?

No, that's not it.

What about the box of Ferrero Rocher you got in the garage when you remembered her birthday at the last minute?

No, 'fraid not.

Well, how about the frilly crotchless panties you plucked up the courage to buy?

Nah, nah and thrice nah.

And it's not just that you're not famous. Even if you cut off your right bollock (and I'd advise against it), it wouldn't begin to compare to some of the truly exotic love offerings in history.

On that basis, nor does Bill Clinton's gift of a Gap dress to Monica Lewinsky (even if he had thoughtfully 'autographed' other items of her clothing).

No, it's got to be more special, more extraordinary.

As the late Dame Barbara Cartland (whom I had the misfortune to meet: believe me, she lived up to her reputation of 'cruelty without beauty') said, 'Tokens are about remembering a person. It's all part of real love.'

So how about Richard Burton buying Elizabeth Taylor the Krupp diamond and various other unbelievably expensive trinkets (as well as marrying her twice), or Chris Evans buying Billie Piper an expensive motor?

Well, they're close but, as Monica would vouchsafe, no cigar.

Ultimately, we're not talking about the sort of present that money can buy. So let me, in reverse order, give you the top exotic love offerings:

In third place is Emperor Shah Jahan, who built the Taj Mahal in memory of his favourite wife.

In second position is Cleopatra, who once dropped two extremely valuable pearls into a glass of wine and drank a toast to Mark Antony; he gave her Cyprus.

But the number one has to be Herod, who gave Salome the head of John the Baptist – just because she asked for it. Now how romantic was that?

Even though the Ferrero Rocher would have been a lot more enjoyable.

How old is too old?

(And when old folk meet each other in an old folks' home and decide to get married, do they consummate the marriage?)

Sometimes this research/writing malarkey is harder than it looks. I mean, you'd probably think that all I'd have to do to get an answer to this question would be to pop down to the local old folks' home and ask a few coffin dodgers whether they still …

WHAT????????????

Is it too late to change careers – or, at the very least, book titles? Something less scary, like *How to Wrestle Man-eating Crocodiles*. Gritting my teeth, I phoned the National Care Association, who, no doubt through equally gritted teeth, told me it was 'down to the individuals'.

Well, thanks a million, guys.

So how old is 'past it'?

I am, I suppose, obliged to say 'never'. But that's not *strictly* true, is it? I mean, 'past it' is when you can't or won't do it any longer or, more likely, when you can't find someone to do it with.

As a man approaching 50, I have a sort of interest in the subject.

I plucked up the courage to ask a friend from the bridge club – a septuagenarian herself – who does a lot of voluntary work with the elderly. To my relief, she wasn't shocked but giggled and told me that she very much doubted whether any of 'her' old people were still 'enjoying sexual relations'.

I told her I hadn't asked whether they were 'enjoying' them but whether they were still having them.

She giggled again and shook her head. 'There are probably a few people but I think by the time you get into your late 70s or 80s, any intimacy is restricted to cuddles – that sort of thing.'

So I did a bit of research and came up with a number of famous people who were still sexually active in their 70s and beyond.

H.G. Wells, Mao Tse-Tung, Bertrand Russell, Victor Hugo, Brigham Young, Benjamin Franklin, Leopold Stokowski, Johann von Goethe (who proposed to a 19-year-old when he was in his 70s), Colette, Leo Tolstoy, Sarah Bernhardt, W. Somerset Maugham, Franz Liszt and King Louis XIV.

But then I thought that just listing people who were sexually active at an advanced age was a little imprecise, so I compiled a list of famous men who fathered children after the age of 60.

Sir John Mortimer (61)	**James Brown (67)**	**Charlie Chaplin (73)**
Sir David Jason (61)	**Yves Montand (67)**	**James Doohan (80)**
Cary Grant (62)	**Pablo Picasso (68)**	**Anthony Quinn (81)**
Clint Eastwood (63)	**Francisco de Goya (68)**	**Saul Bellow (84)**
Marlon Brando (65)	**Lord Snowdon (68)**	
Harvey Keitel (65)	**Des O'Connor (72)**	

It should be noted, however, that in every case their partners were a lot younger.

How young is too young?

I'd say under 16 – which happens to be the British age of sexual consent. Now, come on, Mitch, are you sure? Girls mature much quicker than they did in the past, when the age was set. Isn't there an argument for the age to be changed?

All right then, let's make it 18.

I'm not joking – and to prove it I'll stop having a conversation with myself and address the question seriously. Yes, I know that girls' – and boys' too for that matter – bodies are maturing more quickly but that doesn't mean that they're more mature emotionally or intellectually.

In fact, I think there's a very good argument for making the age of sexual consent 18 – if only to protect younger people from much older predators. The law should work on a common-sense basis. Society can't stop a pair of 17-year-olds – of whatever sexual persuasion – from getting it on and nor should it try to. Even a pair of 15-year-olds shouldn't necessarily be stopped from doing what comes naturally (although a little sex education and a lot more parental responsibility wouldn't go amiss).

However, a particularly sheltered, innocent, immature 17-year-old might need protection from a particularly rapacious 45-year-old (note that I haven't specified gender or sexuality), and that is where the law could and, in my opinion, should operate.

Look, I'm not saying that people only become attractive *after* some arbitrary age of consent. I'm saying that they need protecting until that age. In an era where young girls – aided and abetted by parents who should know better – flaunt their precocious sexuality, it can be confusing for men (especially when women in their 20s and 30s are simultaneously dressing as young girls).

The point is that the law has to set limits. Rightly or wrongly, 18 is the age of majority, of adulthood. I think it makes sense to extend that age to all acts (aye, including smoking and buying lottery tickets) of an adult nature, and what could be more adult than having sex?

Having said all that, I'm aware that I might be merely reflecting contemporary values. Consider these historical characters who all had sex with (what today would be) underage girls: Paul Gauguin (who married – at different times – *three* 14-year-old girls), Sir Charles Chaplin (whose catchphrase was 'the younger the better'), Samuel Pepys, John Barrymore, Howard Hughes, the Marquis de Sade, Errol Flynn and Fyodor Dostoevsky. Consider also Lewis Carroll (who didn't actually do anything to little girls but seems to have had an inordinate interest in them), John Ruskin (who became infatuated with a nine-year-old girl when he was 40) and Emile Zola (who, in his middle age, fantasized about pre-pubescent girls).

Is it true that Orthodox Jews have to have sex through a sheet?

Although I'm Jewish, I don't actually know any Orthodox Jews – and they would certainly have nothing to do with someone as ungodly as me. The fact is that I'm what is known as a 'secular Jew' – although I prefer the expression 'Jewish atheist', which I would qualify by saying that Judaism is the only religion to permit such an oxymoron.

However, I'm not only irreligious, I'm actually anti-religion: I've got no time for it whatsoever and I regard fundamentalists – of any persuasion – to be mad and dangerous in equal measure.

Jewish fundamentalists are – at least outside Israel – more mad than dangerous. You want proof of their madness? OK, the laws of Kashrut (that's kosher to you) demand that meat and milk are never consumed together. Fair enough – as anyone who's had a bellyache from eating a hamburger washed down by a chocolate milkshake will confirm. There might even be a good dietary argument to be made in favour of not having milk in your coffee *after* finishing your meal.

But what about separating the crockery used for milk and meat dishes? And what about – and this is where madness really does creep in – having two dishwashers: one for milk crockery and the other for meat crockery?

But then, of course, it has absolutely nothing whatsoever to do with whatever the original rule was designed to address and everything to do with blind obedience.

So do they have sex through sheets (so that the man won't come into too much direct contact with the woman)? It wouldn't surprise me. After all, I do know for a fact that an Orthodox Jewish man is obliged to forgo any physical (even non-sexual) contact with his wife while she's having her period, so it might even be logical for him to whip out a sheet when the mood takes him.

I said at the beginning that I didn't know the answer to this question but the truth is I'd always believed it to be the case. Sadly, it turns out the wish was father to the thought – even though I am, by all accounts, not the only person to labour under this misapprehension.

Rabbi Jonathan Romain is a leading figure in Reform (i.e. sensible) Judaism. He's also someone I've known and respected ever since the days when we were teenagers and he was a groovy guy known as 'Cat Romain'. These days, he dispenses eminently wise advice to the readers of the *Jewish Chronicle*. So it made sense for me to consult him.

'No, they don't,' he said with a chuckle.

Really? I replied plaintively, as if he might change his answer – just for me.

'No, it's a myth.'

Damn it!

'I tell you what though, they certainly have a lot of children, as many as twelve or thirteen.'

But not conceived through a sheet?

'No.'

Shame.

'Here's something for you to consider. There is a time of the week – on a Friday night – when Jews are actively encouraged to have sex.'

I pricked up my ears – silence at the back there.

Well, that's God and you and me convinced. Now all I have to do is persuade Mrs Symons.

I knew I should have married a Jewish girl – but then she wouldn't have mown the lawn or fixed the roof.

Why is a red light used to represent prostitution?

This practice goes back to the US in the late 19th century where prostitutes would place a red light in their window to attract potential customers.

But why?

There are two theories – either of which (or both) could be true.

The first goes back to the Old Testament of the Bible (so that's why they call it the oldest profession). When Joshua was trying to capture Jericho, he was helped by Rahab, a Jericho prostitute, who identified her house with a scarlet thread. This was, of course, before the walls came tumbling down.

The second theory is that it comes from the red lanterns carried by railroad workers, which they left outside the brothels when they went inside.

My instinct is that neither of these two explanations is true (even though they happened). The Biblical story goes back too far for such a (relatively) modern practice while the railroad workers' lanterns doesn't make sense as red would have become the colour to indicate that a prostitute *wasn't* available.

The best guess is that one or two working girls decided to 'put on the red light' (© Sting) because they'd told clients that that would show they were 'on duty' that night and the practice spread.

And why red? Because it's the universal colour of passion and sex.

Is it true that the Vatican has the greatest collection of pornography in the world?

When I told friends I was writing this book, I asked for any questions they might have on the subject. This one – from Clive (thanks, mate) – came right out of left field.

It couldn't be true, could it?

And yet, I had just enough suspicion to find out one way or the other.

Alas, it wasn't true. And I so wanted it to be!

However, Clive wasn't entirely stupid for asking because there is something of an urban myth surrounding the Vatican and pornography.

It turns out that it came from a throwaway remark by the renowned sexologist Alfred Kinsey, who apparently told his students that he had the greatest collection of pornography – second only to the Vatican's.

It was a joke. JOKE. But, as with so many of these things, it spread (helped in recent years by, you've guessed it, the internet).

By the way, guess who does have the world's largest collection of pornography ...

Yes, that's right – it's the Kinsey Institute in Bloomington, Indiana.

In a threesome, is there an etiquette to deciding which way to turn?

Despite some serious pleading with a girl I used to go out with in my early 20s, I have never known the joys – or otherwise – of three-in-a-bed. Nowadays, as a happily married man, I feel lucky to participate in a two-in-a-bed romp. Give it a few years, and I'll be only too delighted if I can stage a one-in-a-bed tryst. Such is life.

It was time to put in a call to Rick the satyr.

'Sure, I've had threesomes,' he said with enviable coolness. 'Who hasn't?'

Well …

'Basically, everyone except you, Mitch.'

Hang on!

'No, I'm just breaking your balls! Threesomes can be fun or they can be a pain – just like regular sex. The one thing I would say is that when it works well, there's nothing better than a threesome, but when it's bad, it's the absolute pits. That goes double when you're drunk – which is, of course, how most people end up in threesomes in the first place.

'The best ones are the planned ones and the best combo is two guys and one girl.'

You are joking! I didn't take you for a gayboy!

'For a what? Don't be a tosser – or at least no more than you really can't help. Look, moron, a woman can come an unlimited number of times and has three orifices so, like, you do the math.'

Maths.

'What?'

It's 'maths' with an 's' in this country.

'Sor-ry,' he said, not meaning it.

OK, I take on board what you're saying but surely it's more fun for a bloke to have two girls, eh?

'God, you are so fucking bourgeois!'

I ignored him. So how do you know which way to turn? Is there an etiquette?

'What does it matter?'

Come on, Rick.

'All right. Look, if it's your girlfriend who's set up the threesome, don't devote all your attention to her friend. That goes double if the friend's cuter than your girlfriend. Make sure you look after both of them – though you look like someone who'd have difficulty looking after just one of them.

'If you're with two girls, *don't* start trying to manipulate them – you're not a fucking film director – and don't start telling them about your fantasies. Well, at least not unless they ask. Above all, *don't* discriminate between the two.'

How do you mean?

'I mean, don't go down on one and not on the other – just because you don't fancy her so much.'

Thanks, I'll bear it all in mind for ... for ... for ... the afterlife.

'I believe that sex is a beautiful thing between two people. Between FIVE, it's fantastic ... '

Woody Allen

Are there any countries that don't restrict gays from the military?

Before I answer the question, let's make it perfectly clear that throughout history, gays – aye, and lesbians too – have served with distinction in the armed forces.

Many gay men were killed on active service in both world wars and in wars and conflicts ever since.

Rupert Brooke, T.E. Lawrence (of Arabia), Alexander the Great, King Richard I (the Lionheart), Julius Caesar, Pompey and Siegfried Sassoon were all gay or bisexual – as we understand the terms today – and no one could dispute their fighting prowess.

Although military and naval authorities have always frowned upon homosexuality (and, indeed, being openly gay was usually enough to earn a soldier in most militaries a dishonourable discharge), on the ground – in the field and on ships – attitudes have traditionally been more flexible.

As a soldier friend of mine explained: 'As a soldier, you necessarily form attachments with other soldiers. These can be deep friendships and the well-being of the army depends on men having two, three or four muckers who will look out for each other. In wars – especially when non-professionals join the army – these relationships can sometimes be sexual or quasi-sexual as well. That was certainly the case in World War Two where some couples were openly gay. However, for the most part, it works on the basis of "don't ask, don't tell".'

That was the Clinton line, wasn't it?

'Yes. The other line that came from that era was "soldiers don't want to take showers with men who want to take showers with soldiers" but, in fact, you'll find that soldiers are, in some ways, more tolerant than the rest of the population. If a bloke's popular and well respected then the fact that he's gay won't necessarily prejudice them against him.

'As for the navy, they didn't call it "rum, sodomy and the lash" for nothing, you know.'

Further research shows that Australia, Austria, Belgium, Canada, the Czech Republic, Denmark, Estonia, France, Germany, Ireland, Israel, Japan, the Netherlands, Norway, Spain, Sweden and the UK all allow gays and lesbians to serve in the armed forces.

Greece, Hungary, Italy and Turkey actually ban gays from serving in the armed forces. The situation in Russia and other former Soviet Union countries is less clear. Since 2003, however, 'well-adjusted' gays and lesbians have been allowed to serve in the Russian army (though that probably has more to do with a shortage of recruits than a shift in attitude).

Third world countries – particularly in Africa – are as antagonistic towards homosexuals in the army as they are to homosexuals in civilian life.

Does sex cure boys' acne or is it just that boys lose their spots at the same time as they lose their virginity?

I confess that I hadn't heard of this rumour – not even during my own adolescence – but then I suppose I was lucky enough not to suffer the curse of acne.

Mind you, the first lad in my crowd to pop his cherry did, in fact, have the worst acne of all of us – even after he'd 'done it' six times (he kept us up to date with his progress and was decent enough to inform us that you weren't a man until you had done it six times – which was handy for him).

Nevertheless – or do I mean nonetheless, and what, indeed, is the difference? – as I've had reason to remark before, what do I know?

Someone, however, who should know is my old pal (well, more of an acquaintance if truth be told), Dr Roland Powell, who for once wasn't so forbearing when I asked him whether sex cured acne.

'No,' he said somewhat testily (if testily means what I think it means – and you can't be too careful), 'having vaginal intercourse does not cure acne.'

Oh, OK. Well, that's it then. Perhaps the rest of the book can be completed in a series of yes/no answers. It'd save time but might possibly turn out a bit boring.

So, Doctor, is there a syllogism at work here? Is it that boys lose their spots at roughly the same time as they lose their virginity but the two are otherwise unconnected?

'I know what a syllogism is, thank you very much,' he replied, still somewhat testily. 'I suppose so. What is beyond doubt is that acne is a common side effect of puberty – usually on the face—'

Isn't nature a bitch?

'It's also true that the acne is caused by an increase in testosterone, an androgen. Androgens are also partly responsible for an increase in the oil – or sebum – produced by the sebaceous glands in the skin, which, when affected by bacteria, lead to acne. When the hormonal changes of puberty end – so too does acne. Or at least usually. We're talking about the age of 16, 17 and 18.'

In other words, the precise age that most people have sex for the first time.

'Exactly. The other connection between the two is that a youth with a face full of spots is unlikely to appeal to a girl so he might have to wait until his face clears before he can experience sex.'

Is it possible for men to fake orgasm?

Difficult one, this. Unlike a female orgasm, which doesn't (or, at least, not necessarily) produce physical evidence, the male orgasm does.

Trouble is that the answer obliges me to reveal more about myself than I'd rather. Because how can I, in all conscience, consult an expert when I know the answer to the question is yes.

You know the problem that some men have with premature ejaculation? Well, I used to suffer from the opposite. Sometimes, it would take me forever to achieve a climax and, yes, on some occasions when I didn't think I would get there, I would pretend that I'd come.

'You haven't come,' said one girl when I'd stopped.

'Yes I have.'

'That's very strange, I didn't feel anything … '

Cue one very embarrassed teenage boy.

At this stage, I should point out that those halcyon days of multiple partners fell post-pill and pre-AIDS. Consequently, this largely obviated the need for condoms. Taking care of contraception consisted of saying to one's partner, 'You are on the pill, aren't you?'

UUuuuunnnnnnn

yesyes..yesssss

Anyway, this explains just why girls could tell if their blokes had indeed reached their climaxes.

Obviously, using a condom would have allowed for any amount of subterfuge and deception but condoms were as alien to us as 'unsafe sex' is to my sons' generation. Or so I hope.

Eventually, by the time I reached my early 20s, I realized that I had a problem that was simply caused by a mixture of nerves and – incredible as this will sound to any of my subsequent lovers – an inability to concentrate on my own pleasure. In other words, I would be so pathetically grateful to any girl who'd allow me to do press-ups on her that I would devote myself to giving her a good time. I remember one girl who had eight orgasms to my, er, nought. Hey, now I understand why she used to pester me for years after.

Fortunately – for me, if not for my partners – I learned to achieve an orgasm during sex with others as I did in all my solo encounters. In other words, I could reproduce my training-pitch form in the big match.

So, to answer the question – if only from my own necessarily limited experience – I'd say that, yes, men can fake orgasms but not the physical proof …

135

Can a man be raped by a woman?

There's an old saying to the effect that an erect penis has no conscience – but does it have a choice? That's the nub of this question.

Obviously now with Viagra, a man can have an erection of which a woman who has managed to subdue him (or, at least, the rest of his body) can take full advantage without his consent. That would clearly be a case of rape.

Before then, it was much harder for a woman to rape a man and even harder to prove it.

There have been isolated reports – and urban myths – of young men brought to erection by attractive girls and then having a tourniquet wrapped around their penises which are then used by older, uglier women for intercourse. These 'incidents' invariably take place in faraway countries as initiation ceremonies or as punishments for lewd behaviour and should, for the most part, be treated as cautionary tales.

Much more common – and real – are instances where women have drugged, blackmailed and/or physically threatened men into non-consensual sex.

Here the argument against the plausibility of a woman raping a man always went that even if a woman was threatening that man with a gun, he wouldn't be able to penetrate her unless he achieved an erection – in other words, even if he didn't consent, his penis did.

That strikes me as a specious argument.

Would you say that a woman threatened with a gun isn't being raped if she becomes sexually aroused to the point of lubrication?

Of course not. It's a question of consent.

However extreme seduction might be, there is always a real dividing line between that and coercion.

The (in)famous case of Joyce McKinney illustrates this perfectly.

McKinney was a former Miss Wyoming who joined the Mormons and began a relationship with a young missionary named Kirk Anderson. He ended it but she continued to pursue him. In 1977, he moved to London but, with the help of a private detective, McKinney tracked him down and, helped by Keith May, a man who was in turn infatuated with her, kidnapped Anderson and took him to a cottage where he was held for three days.

During that time, McKinney and May tied down Anderson's arms and legs with leather straps, padlocks, rope and chains so that Anderson was spreadeagled on a bed. May left the room and then, according to Anderson, McKinney 'grabbed my pyjamas from just around my neck and tore them from my body. The chains were tight and I could not move. She proceeded to have intercourse. I did not want it to happen. I was very upset.'

McKinney countered this by saying, 'Kirk has to be tied up to have an orgasm. I cooperated because I loved him and wanted to help him. Sexual bondage turns him on because he doesn't have to feel guilty. The thought of being powerless before a woman seems to excite him. I didn't have to give him oral sex ... I did do it at his request because he likes it.'

Then, in a sentence that kept satirists and comedians in material for the rest of the 1970s, she added, 'I loved Kirk so much that I would have skied down Mount Everest in the nude with a carnation up my nose.'

McKinney was charged with kidnapping – because it was then impossible for a woman to be charged with raping a man – and given bail to reappear at her trial, which was due to start in May of the following year.

Guess what? She didn't turn up. In her absence, she was eventually sentenced to a year's imprisonment.

But not for rape.

I remember the case well. As a man of the same age as Kirk Anderson, I was mightily amused – and not a little aroused – by the thought of a man being thus coerced by a not unattractive woman (ridiculously upturned nose as I recall).

That was then, this is now.

These days, we know better.

Don't we?

Is it true that Eskimo men lend their wives to strangers?

Have you ever heard of this one? I had and, I have to say, it was quite a cherished fantasy – until, that is, I actually caught sight of some photos of Eskimo (or, as we now call them, Inuit) women.

Er, no thanks …

They say that people adapt to their conditions. So that while people who live in the Sahara desert are tall and thin, people who live in and around snow tend to be short and squat.

Not my type, I'm afraid.

Still, there was no reason why it might not be true – especially as Eskimos are renowned for their hospitality and, well, it is jolly cold in the Arctic. Hence the adjective 'arctic'.

Once again, I turned to my favourite – not to say my *only* – social anthropologist, Dr Lorraine Mackintosh.

'Sorry to disappoint you, Mitch, but it's not really true.'

Not really? That suggests that there's something in it.

'Well, using the word Eskimo as a broad term for all the people who live in the extreme north, it is true to say that, traditionally, they had slightly different marital arrangements to other contemporary groups. For example, they went in for what might be called "spousal exchange".'

Wife-swapping?

'Sort of, but it was usually tied in with religious ceremonies. And sometimes these arrangements went much further and developed into a sort of co-marriage in which families were joined together.'

So there was no wife-lending to strangers?

'Only rarely and certainly not nowadays. I believe that a Danish explorer named Mikkelsen wrote of being offered an Eskimo's wife but this was probably because of the cold. Nevertheless, his account of the offer fed the legend – along with two other things: Eskimos' unorthodox – to us – marital arrangements and the fact that Eskimo men were renowned for their hospitality.'

Why are gay men called 'fags'?

The British and the Americans are, of course, two peoples separated by a common language.

Nowhere is this more evident than when it comes to the word 'fag'.

You see, to we Brits, the word means either a cigarette or a young schoolboy who performs menial duties for an older boy – you can see a possible derivation already. Also, the word faggot is used to describe a British meatball served in gravy.

Nowadays, of course, fagging (where schoolboys serve other schoolboys) no longer takes place in schools – and, indeed, the consumption of fags (in the sense of cigarettes) is also down. And who eats faggots any more (who indeed?)?

But fags, as in a rude word to describe gay men, what's the origin of that?

I decided to consult Dr Karen Landy (who is, incidentally, halfway to being a fag-hag: yup, she's a hag).

'If you go back to the origins of the word "faggot", you'll find that it refers to a bundle of sticks or branches.'

OK but how do you get from there to gays?

'Patience, patience, you have none. It was thought that there was a connection because homosexual men were burned at the stake and the fire would have been started with a bundle of sticks. However, this is unlikely, since this was a British practice and the use of the word "faggot" or "fag" to mean a homosexual man is American in origin. However, if we can stay on this side of the Atlantic for a moment, there are other clues to the derivation of this usage. Butchers would throw the "faggot-end of meat" into the gutters; consequently, street prostitutes became known as "faggots".'

Female prostitutes?

'Yes. Also in Britain – in northern England – the word faggot was used to describe a stupid (in the sense of idiotic) person. So it's possible to see the beginnings of a derivation in—'

Is it?

'Look, not all definitions and origins are clear-cut – especially when it comes to slang. Sometimes, there are many separate roots that come together to produce a word in common currency. The word "faggot" is a case in point. It has a certain onomatopoeic quality, don't you think?'

I suppose so.

'Faggot would have been just one in a series of words used to describe homosexuals at a time – America in the 1920s – when the practice was still illegal but more and more men were displaying their sexuality. Other such words were "queer" and "fairy" and "queen", and, interestingly, gay men would use them themselves to describe different types of gays – much in the same way as they would nowadays describe one another as "butch" or "straight-looking" or whatever.'

So that's it then? It just evolved into its pejorative meaning from a series of different routes?

'Pretty much so. I'm sorry I can't be more specific.'

You're sorry ... Where does 'fag' as in the sense of cigarette fit in? Is there a connection with 'faggot'?

'No, the leftover bit of a piece of cloth was known as a "fag-end". From there, you have the leftover bit of a cigarette being called a fag-end and then the word "fag" – not unreasonably – became used as a slang word for cigarette.'

And fag – as in one schoolboy looking after another – surely that has a link into gay practices?

'You'd have thought so but no, it comes from the notion that the person performing the task became fagged out – or tired – as a result of having to work hard.'

Well, I'm definitely fagged out with this question.

Does the G-spot really exist?

You won't be surprised to know that this isn't really my territory. Although I'm old enough to remember the excitement of the 'discovery' of the G-spot, I had quite enough trouble remembering the clitoris – let alone engaging with a whole new erogenous zone.

Yup, that's the kind of lover I am.

But after all the fuss of the 1980s, did it even exist at all?

For the answer to that, we have to go back to the eponymous Dr Ernest Grafenberg, a gynaecologist who in 1950 wrote an article about the sensitivity of the anterior vaginal wall.

This is where the G-spot (named after Dr G. in a 1982 book entitled *The G Spot and Other Recent Discoveries About Human Sexuality*) is supposedly located.

To be specific, it is said to be a sexually sensitive small area on the upper wall of the vagina approximately two inches from the opening and close to the bladder and urethra.

The 'discovery' of this spot led to a sort of vaginal gold rush as the women of the Western world shucked off their shoulder pads and – sometimes with the help of their menfolk – dedicated themselves to the task of finding this magic button.

Some were successful but many were not and struggled to see what the fuss was all about.

Scientists were equally divided. Some said it was the key to female ejaculation and proved that Freud had been right all along with his distinction between the vaginal and the clitoral orgasm; others disagreed and pointed to an absence of necessary nerve endings.

Interestingly, although Grafenberg himself made orgasmic claims for the importance of the area that would eventually bear his name, he also said, 'There is no spot in the female body from which sexual desire could not be aroused. Innumerable erotogenic spots are distributed all over the body, from where sexual satisfaction can be elicited; these are so many that we can almost say that there is no part of the female body which does not give sexual response, the partner has only to find the erotogenic zones.'

So there you have it. For those women who've found their G-spot, it definitely exists; for those who haven't, it doesn't.

Do gynaecologists make better lovers?

Now that I come to answer this question, I've just realized that there's an inherent assumption in it that all gynaecologists are men.

In fact, six out of seven gynaecologists are men – which makes it pretty overwhelmingly male as professions go – but not entirely so.

Anyway, that quibble aside, let's assume that the question refers to male gynaecologists.

I don't know any gynaecologists and nor do I know anyone who's married to one. Fortunately, my wife is acquainted with two women who are or were married to gynaecologists. One is married to a consultant gynaecologist who operates out of Harley Street. She says that he's brilliant when it comes to diagnosing things – and that was especially true during her three pregnancies – but that he was a tad unsympathetic with her routine gynaecological problems. Is he a good lover, asked my wife. Apparently, yes he is.

The other woman is now divorced and told my wife that he was a lousy lover – always had been even when they were first together.

So what can we deduce from this 'evidence'? That gynaecologists are better or worse lovers?

I don't think so.

No, what we can conclude is that a happily married woman says that her husband is a good lover (whether or not he is) and that a happily divorced woman reckons that her ex-husband is a bad lover (whether or not he was).

C'est la vie.

All one can say with any degree of certainty is that, unlike the rest of their gender, male gynaecologists will have a better idea of physiology. Whether this makes them better lovers is debatable but at least it means they know what they're doing (good or bad) and where they're going.

Meanwhile, a recent survey revealed that as many as a third of American gynaecologists reckon that their sex life is adversely affected by their work. And a British gynaecologist was quoted in the papers as saying, 'You see so many vaginas during the normal course of a working day that when we leave work we just want to have a rest from them. I suppose it's a bit like a porn star.'

Er, not quite, mate – but we take your point.

Which leaves me with a question to which there isn't an answer: why does a gynaecologist leave the room when his patient is undressing?

Why do gentlemen prefer blondes?

There seems to be little doubt that men – never mind gentlemen – find blondes sexy. If you don't believe me then ask any blonde-by-choice woman (aka 'bottle blonde') whether she gets more wolf-whistles when she's blonde or when she's not and she'll tell you in no uncertain terms that blondes have more fun.

Always supposing, that is, that their idea of fun is being whistled at by Neanderthals displaying acres of bum cleavage.

So why is it?

Could it be the paucity of blondes? After all, only 2 per cent of the human race is genuinely fair.

Perhaps, but paucity in itself is unlikely to be the cause or else we'd all be gagging for people with hare-lips or incredible overbites.

More likely, there's a question of cause and effect at work here. Since it is widely accepted – in the West at least – that men find blonde women sexier than other women, then the moment a woman dyes her hair blonde, she is making a statement (consciously or unconsciously) that she wishes to look sexier. And so it goes.

But that still doesn't answer the question of why men prefer blondes. I decided to consult my favourite anthropologist, Dr Lorraine Mackintosh, who is herself a blonde (though, I suspect, not a natural one).

'I don't think it's the shortage of natural blondes that causes men to find them attractive but the fact that they look so striking. If you look at other species, you'll see that when creatures of either sex have a choice of mate, they tend to pick one that looks exciting and different: just look at the peacock. Why should humans be any different?

'I also take your point about women choosing to be blonde and sending out certain signals. Again, if we return to the animal kingdom, the idea is that a creature is putting out a signal that, effectively, says, "Look at me, I'm in such good condition that I can afford to care about how I look."'

And you look fine.

'I was a genuine blonde in my youth, believe me! Almost white, I was.'

I believe you. What happened? I mean …

'I grew out of it. The way it works is that if all fourteen of your parents, grandparents, great-grandparents etc. were blonde then you will be too for all your life, but the more of them who weren't blonde, the less likely it is that you will remain blonde.'

And do gentlemen prefer blondes?

'Yes, in societies where they are still naturally rare, but there's every reason to believe that if there were a society which was almost exclusively composed of blondes, then men would fight over brunettes.'

So, in the kingdom of the natural blonde, the mouse is queen?

'That's right!'

Is there anyone in contact ad-land who isn't 'attractive' or doesn't possess a 'GSOH'?

I've never placed a contact ad – honest – and I've only ever answered one on one occasion, but when I tell you what happened, you'll understand why I was never tempted to repeat the experience.

It was back in 1979, when I was young, free and single. One day, I saw an ad in the London listings magazine *Time Out* that went something along the lines of: 'Beautiful blonde damsel in distress seeks knight on white steed to rescue her.'

I was curious and bored and so I sent a reply – saying that I didn't have a white steed but I did have a white Morris Marina.

Some time later, I got a call from a nice-sounding girl. Of course, in those days, I hadn't yet heard the important advice: 'If they sound cute on the phone, add three stone.'

So off I went in my white Morris Marina and, a couple of hours later, arrived at the girl's door.

Oh dear, oh dear, oh dear.

She was not (as I'd assumed from the phone conversation) the same sort of age as me (22); she was also most definitely *not* cute. I'd say mid-30s, seriously overweight and, not to put too fine a point on it, ugly.

To my credit, I stayed for a few hours before making my excuses – but not before I asked her (as discreetly as I could) about the wording of her ad.

'Oh, that,' she says, 'that was a Christmas present from my friends.'

'Ah,' says I, 'so it was they who described you as a "beautiful blonde damsel"?'

'Yes, wasn't that nice of them?'

I smiled through gritted teeth while calculating a) how soon I could leave and b) whether I had a case against her bloody friends under the Trade Descriptions Act.

So, my experience of lonely hearts ads is what you might call 'jaundiced'.

Still, there's clearly a market for them, as you can see from all the newspapers and magazines that run them.

Look, I'm happily married – as we've already established – but that doesn't mean that I don't occasionally peruse these ads (I'm also happy with my car but that doesn't stop me reading motoring magazines).

And, yes, everyone in contact ad-land really does seem to be attractive and in possession of a Good Sense Of Humour.

Which, of course, begs the question: how come they need to advertise?

CUDDLE UP CLOSE
Slim, easy-going guy, 42, GSOH, seeks homely, friendly F for laughs & cuddles.

A CALL FROM THE TALL
Tall, slim, attractive, fun-loving F, 44, looking to meet M for fun times & long-term relationship. SW Ldn.

LOOKING TO SETTLE DOWN
Fit, athletic, fun-loving M, young 37, 6', likes days out, pubs, clubs & socialising. Seeks looking slim F, 25-35, genuine, caring, for long-t relationship. GSOH, for long-t

ADVENTUROUS MANAGING DIRECTOR
Solvent, semi-retired M, 62, 5'7", world traveller, no ties, pony-tailed, seeks unconventional, sponataneous, slim, tactile F, 38-50, any race, for relationship

Just as I was proposing to delve deeper into this issue, a 'funny' arrived in my email inbox that answers the question of why there seems to be such a gap between what people say of themselves and the (sadder) truth.

Here then is how those contact ad buzzwords translate.

40-ish	49
Adventurous	Slept with everyone
Athletic	No breasts
Average-looking	Moooo
Beautiful	Pathological liar
Emotionally secure	On medication
Feminist	Fat
Free spirit	Junkie
Friendship first	Former slut
Huggable	Hugely fat
New Age	Body hair in the wrong places
Old-fashioned	No BJs
Open-minded	Desperate
Outgoing	Loud and embarrassing
Professional	Bitch
Voluptuous	Very fat
Wants soulmate	Stalker

Are transvestites more or less likely to be gay?

The answer, according to a friend of a friend who occasionally likes to get into women's clothes (when they're *not* wearing them), is 'almost universally heterosexual'.

I was astonished, as I'd always kind of assumed that men who wore women's clothes were, in some way, heading past the centre point on the straight–gay continuum.

'No,' said my friend's friend who, for reasons that are obvious but which still shame the society in which we live, asked to remain anonymous, 'not at all. If anything, there's an argument that says that because we have an outlet for our feminine side, then we're much *more* straight than other heterosexual men.'

Blimey!

'I wear dresses and put on make-up because I enjoy the experience. I rarely do so outside the house because it carries so much stigma. At home with my wife, however, is entirely different and we have a lot of fun dressing me up and making me up etc.'

So your wife doesn't mind?

'Mind? She loves it! We have our very best sex before, during and after. You should try it!'

No thanks – it's never appealed.

'Fair enough, but you shouldn't knock it till you've tried it.'

I'm not being coy here: the idea of getting into a frock (as opposed to getting into a woman's knickers) doesn't do anything for me. However, as with all such things, I'm intrigued to know how someone discovers it for the first time.

'I've been cross-dressing since I was old enough to walk into my mum's room and try on her clothes. I never got off on it or anything, I just enjoyed the experience and the thrill of doing something just a little naughty. When I left home and moved into my own place, I kept a few items of clothing I'd bought from charity shops for dressing up in. When I met my girlfriend – who's now my wife – I told her about it and she was absolutely fine.'

What if she hadn't been?

'Then she probably wouldn't have become my wife.'

It's that important?

'Yes and no. I don't do it often but it's still an important part of me and I don't think I could have ended up with someone who disapproved of it. I guess if she'd perhaps only tolerated it, it would have been OK, but, as it is, it's fabulous.'

Can animals get sexually transmitted diseases (STDs)?

Yes, according to my pal Lucy, a zoologist (who, as we sip herbal tea, points out to me that the word 'zoology' logically ought to be pronounced 'zo-ology' rather than 'zoo-ology').

'STDs occur throughout the animal kingdom.'

Which animals can get them?

'You name them.'

You're the zoologist – sorry, zo-ologist – you name them.

'Horses, dogs, koalas, rabbits … even snails. However, they're more prevalent in domestic animals than in animals that live in the wild.'

Why?

'Because for STDs to spread, it requires a lot of mating and there's less mating – less proximity – in the wild.'

What's the effect on animals?

'STDs can cause sterility in animals. In doing so, they end up controlling the population of affected breeds. Is there cause and effect? We just don't know. What we do know is that they can have an immense bearing on those animal groups where a small number of males mate with huge numbers of females. It's called "harem mating" and it makes it easier for the disease's organisms to spread because these organisms are actually pretty frail.'

Tell me, Lucy, can STDs be passed from humans to animals – or, indeed, the other way round?

She smiled.

No, no, no, I wasn't thinking of myself …

'Methink you do protest too much …'

Don't be silly and answer the bloody question, girl.

'No, you're all right …'

Not me!

'OK, infected humans who have sex with animals are in no danger of passing on their STD – and vice versa.'

How come?

'Because STDs are what we call species-specific. But, hey, Mitch, you could always try using a condom ...'

What is the origin of the 'c' word?

Despite – no, *because* of – the fact that it's just the most offensive word in the English language (particularly for women), I have to say that the 'c' word is one of my absolute favourite words. It might not be as beautiful as 'royalties' but there are times when it's a lot more useful: when was the last time you called someone 'a complete royalties'?

It's principal meaning is, of course, 'vagina'. However, the world's usefulness lies in its two other pejorative meanings: 'unpleasant person' and 'utter idiot' – as illustrated in the following exchange.

'You're the second biggest cunt in the world.'

'Why only the second biggest?'

'Because you're such a cunt.'

I was going to ask the redoubtable Dr Karen Landy for her help with this one but, you know, sexist old fool that I am, I'm kinda reluctant to discuss this particular word with a woman – even a woman like Dr L., who's as tough an old dragon as ever breathed fire.

So I went through my books and then put the word into Google … and, oh dear, you do get taken to some extraordinary sites. Why, it was at least three hours before I even started on the etymology of the word.

According to the Oxford English Dictionary (OED), the earliest use of the word is in a reference to a street named 'Gropecuntelane'. There were many roads thus named because that's where prostitutes did their business and were, one assumes, 'groped' (they were pretty literal in the Middle Ages).

At that time – and, indeed, up until about the 16th century – the word was merely descriptive of a woman's private parts and not at all offensive. It was used by Chaucer in The Canterbury Tales, but by the time Shakespeare was writing, it was not a word he felt able to use freely (although there are one or two clever puns in his plays).

The word derives from Old German ('kunton') and first appeared in Middle English as 'cunte' (incidentally, there are similar words used to describe female genitalia in other European languages). Although the word comes to us from the Germans, there's also the Latin word 'cunnus' (meaning 'vulva') to consider, but there are, apparently, no etymological links between the two.

The word was not included in any English dictionary from 1795 until Webster's defined it in 1961. The OED followed suit in 1972.

Is it possible to have an orgasm without being touched?

Yes it is! Some people (lucky sods) can achieve orgasms without being touched at all – just from having the right kind of emotional, visual or psychological stimulation. However, this privilege is granted to very few people. According to Kinsey, only three or four men out of the 5,000 in his sample had experienced ejaculation by fantasy alone. That works out at between 0.06 and 0.08 per cent. Interestingly – given that female orgasms are usually more elusive then male – 2 per cent of females in the sample had reached orgasm merely by fantasizing about erotic situations (without any tactile stimulation).

Apparently, it's possible to train yourself to have such orgasms – through exercise and by learning certain types of breathing.

What is the most innocuous song/film/book banned for being too sexual?

In the days when it had a virtual monopoly of all (legal) British radio stations, the BBC could and did ban just about anything on almost any grounds.

While you could (just about) see the reasons for banning songs like 'Je T'Aime (Moi Non Plus)' by Serge Gainsbourg and Jane Birkin (though it was unbelievable that *Top of The Pops* tried to pretend it didn't even exist when it reached the top of the charts), 'God Save The Queen' by the Sex Pistols and George Michael's 'I Want Your Sex', the decision not to play other songs was clearly absurd – even at the time.

Chuck Berry's 'My Ding-A-Ling' was banned because he was singing about his ding-a-ling (and isn't it a crushing indictment of the British music-buying public that this silly little song should provide a rock and roll pioneer with his only UK number one?)

Back in the days before he became Yusuf Islam, Cat Stevens recorded 'I'm Gonna Get Me A Gun' and that too displeased the Beeb.

Perhaps most ludicrous of all was the time that the peerless Ray Davies had to fly back from the US to change the word 'Coca' to 'cherry' in the song 'Lola' because the BBC didn't allow advertising.

This brings me to the nub of the question because it shows what a farce almost all censorship is. While the Beeb was getting its knickers in a twist over the song's references to Coca-Cola, it promptly missed the fact that 'Lola' is a song about a transsexual – which was surely not a subject that the corporation would have considered suitable back in 1970.

Here are some others that slipped through the net:

'Walk On The Wild Side' *(Lou Reed)* There are so many allusions to sex, transvestites and drugs in this 1973 song that it's extraordinary it wasn't banned.

'Pictures of Lily' *(The Who)* A song about the old five-finger shuffle, which no one at the BBC picked up on.

'Blinded By The Light' *(Manfred Mann's Earth Band)* 1976 song – written by Bruce Springsteen – which is also a paean to self-abuse.

'(I Can't Get No) Satisfaction' *(The Rolling Stones)* While Mick and the lads had no end of trouble with 'Let's Spend The Night Together' (having to change the words to 'let's spend some time together'), two years earlier (1965) a song which alluded to a girl's period ('losing streak') had no problem getting through.

'See Emily Play' *(Pink Floyd)* This apparently innocent song reached number 6 in 1967 and received lots of airplay from DJs obviously unaware that the song was all about a girl 'discovering' herself and so is inviting us to indulge in voyeurism. Not the sort of thing the Beeb would have wanted to encourage in the year of 'Puppet On A String'.

'John Wayne Is Big Leggy' *(Haysi Fantayzee)* This 1982 song reached number 11 without anyone in the BBC apparently realizing that it is all about … well, put it this way, 'big leggy' refers to a part of a man that isn't a leg.

While on the subject of songs banned by the BBC, I have a coda to add. On a school trip to the former Soviet Union, we made a short stop in Brest-Litovsk, the Russian border town where the 1917 armistice was signed. We were escorted to the memorial by some charming students who were keen to know all about our Western music. Some of our 20-strong party taunted them and the communist system for banning decadent acts like Slade and Sweet. Revenge was taken when a Russian girl innocently inquired whether we'd heard a record she'd recently bought: 'Give Ireland Back To The Irish' by Wings. No, we were forced to concede, we hadn't: it was banned in Britain.

Do top-shelf magazines discriminate against short men?

My mate Duncan is five foot three. Even taking him at his word (and I suspect that he might be overestimating by an inch or two), he is – to use the modern vernacular – height-challenged.

Mind you, as I tried to reassure him, he's taller than Danny DeVito and Ronnie Corbett and the same height as Mickey Rooney, Bernie Ecclestone and Prince Naseem Hamed.

On the other hand, he's shorter than Michael J. Fox, Roman Polanski, Sachin Tendulkar, Peter Lorre, Joe Pesci, Sanjeev Bhaskar, Martin Amis and Elijah Wood. And let's face it, none of them are giants.

Still, he's a fine fellow and just the person to answer this question. So do top-shelf magazines discriminate against short-arses like him?

'No, you idiot,' he said, giving me a not-so-playful punch in my solar plexus (would have been my throat if he'd been regular size), 'they discriminate against children – which is the whole bloody point. Besides, it's not the magazines that do the discriminating but the shops. Where would you have them keep them? On the counter?'

Yeah, but kidding aside, isn't it unfair on blokes like you?

'You're not kidding aside, are you? Blokes like me – as you so charmingly put it – can jump up or we can ask for assistance.'

From a female shop assistant?

'From another customer – male customer – if we really have to. Personally, I've always queried the need for ordinary newsagents to sell pornography.'

Soft porn.

'Call it what you will: it's designed to arouse, to help blokes wank, no?'

I conceded his point.

'So what's it doing on the high street? That's the question you should be asking.'

All right, so that's the so-called men's magazines. What about the lads' magazines – like *Loaded* and *FHM*?

'Well, they're not on the top shelf, are they?'

I don't know.

Suddenly, it didn't seem to matter as the discussion had moved on.

'I think they're different,' he said after some consideration. 'True, they have lots of naked women in them but I don't think that's the whole point of them, do you?'

Again, I conceded: that such magazines were more about lifestyle – even more so than *Playboy* and *Penthouse* were a generation earlier.

'In any event,' he concluded, 'who pays for porn in a magazine when they can look at it for free on the net? And, before you say anything, Mitch, yes I am tall enough to reach my keyboard.'

What are the signs that your partner's having an affair?

Depends on your partner. Like good poker players, successful adulterers don't provide any tells. Maybe that's why I don't stray, because I'd give it away to my wife. She'd know – immediately.

There are, of course, obvious – not to say clichéd – signs.

He/she's paying too much attention/too little attention; buying more presents/fewer presents; blushing when questioned; proving elusive.

I'd have thought the real tell-tale sign was people being out of contact – especially these days with mobile phones. (Although mobile phones might help adulterers. In the old days, they'd have had to give hotel phone numbers to their partners – which would, of course, indicate where they were – whereas nowadays who knows where someone on a mobile phone might be?)

Try Googling 'having an affair' (as I did) and the first thing you get – or, at least, the first thing I got – is www.illicitencounters.com.

'Married but want a lover?'

There are even dating services for 'attached people', which presumably attract people who reckon they'll be safer cheating with people who've also got something to lose – rather than run the risk of meeting a single bunny-boiler.

On the same Google results page, there were many sponsored links (see opposite). Clearly there's a lot of it about. And you know how you can tell? Because of the volume of commercial advertising the simple question attracted.

Partners lie. Spouses lie. The market never lies.

In the days when homosexuality was illegal, were there any famous men convicted of gay 'crimes'?

Sadly – and ludicrously (in these more enlightened times) – the answer is yes.

Here's a roll-call of just some of the victimized.

Sir John Gielgud. In 1953, the great actor was fined £15 after pleading guilty to a charge of 'importuning' in a public lavatory. In an attempt to avoid publicity, Gielgud listed his occupation as 'clerk'.

Peter Wyngarde. In 1975, the actor best known as Jason King in *Department S* was arrested in a public toilet and accused of committing an act of gross indecency with a Gloucester crane driver. He was fined £75 but, worse, his career nose-dived.

Leonardo da Vinci. The greatest artist of all time was a lifelong homosexual. At the age of 24, he was arrested for going with a 17-year-old male prostitute and was jailed for a short time before his friends could release him.

Montgomery Clift. Just after becoming famous, the actor was arrested for trying to pick up a male prostitute in New York.

Oscar Wilde. As everyone knows, Wilde started a libel case against the Marquess of Queensberry, the father of his lover Lord Alfred Douglas, for calling him a sodomite, which he lost. This led to a criminal trial in which he was sentenced to two years' hard labour in Reading Gaol where he wrote his immortal 'Ballad'.

Alan Turing. The mathematical genius who broke the German Enigma code (and thus helped us to win World War Two) was charged with 'gross indecency' for his relationship with a 19-year-old boy. He was put on probation and given 'treatment' for his homosexuality that was a possible cause of his suicide two years later. His story was brilliantly adapted for the stage by Hugh Whitemore in the play *Breaking The Code,* with Sir Derek Jacobi portraying Turing.

Bill Tilden. The great American tennis player was arrested in 1964 and sent to a California 'honor farm' for 'contributing to the delinquency of a minor'.

Tom Driberg. The former Labour MP and journalist was caught cottaging on more than one occasion but his boss, Lord Beaverbrook, managed to get the charges dropped.

So who was St Valentine?

In ancient Rome, 14 February was deemed to be a holiday to honour Juno, the goddess of women and marriage. The next day was the beginning of the Feast of Lupercalia, during which the names of Roman girls were written down and put into jars. Roman boys would then pick names at random and these couples would be together for the duration of the festival. Inevitably, the way these things go, some of the couples ended up getting married.

I only tell you all this to illustrate the fact that, just like so many other days in the calendar (Easter and Christmas are obvious examples), St Valentine's Day has its roots in pre-Christian times.

However, Valentine himself was undoubtedly a Christian. He was a bishop of Terni, who was martyred in Rome in the third century AD. His crime?

Well, the Emperor Claudius II – known as Claudius the Cruel (remember, the clue's in the name) – was having great difficulty in persuading young men to join the army. He decided that this was because they didn't want to leave their wives and girlfriends and so unilaterally (as cruel emperors are wont to do) he banned marriages and engagements. Valentine, the Bishop of Terni (stray thought for anyone over the age of 40: if Terni had a restaurant serving prawn cocktails, steaks and black forest gateau, it would be a Terni Inn), was having none of it and continued to perform marriages in secret.

When he was discovered, he was condemned to be beaten to death with clubs and to have his head cut off on 14 February 270 (or thereabouts). Not a particularly nice way to go, but he was declared a martyr and then became a saint so I guess it turned out all right in the end. The point is, even if he'd lived to be 100 and died in his bed, he'd be dead by now anyway.

So, thanks to him, every 14 February we send each other mushy cards, buy overpriced flowers and place the most extraordinarily silly personal ads in otherwise sensible newspapers. Or, rather, you might, but Mrs Symons and I don't. For although we are romantically inclined the rest of the year, there is something about St Valentine's Day that brings out the whatever-the-14-February-equivalent-of-Scrooge-is in us and we are resolutely non-lovey-dovey all day long.

As for when this business of cards etc. started, it's reckoned that it was 1477 when one Margery Brews sent a letter to a man named John Paston addressed 'To my right welbelovyd Voluntyne'. This is reckoned to be the oldest known Valentine's card.

Having said that, according to legend, Valentine sent the first 'Valentine' greeting himself. It's said that, while in prison, he fell in love with a young girl – possibly the daughter of the prison warder – who visited him. Just before his death, he wrote her a letter signed 'From your Valentine'. So there you have it. Or not, as the case may be.

Is it true that nurses will 'relieve' a patient who can't oblige himself?

Like most adolescents, I'd heard this from a boy who'd heard it from another boy etc. etc. and then I met someone who told me that it had actually happened to him!

I believed him – oh God I believed him! I believed him night after night until I nearly went blind with belief. Bear in mind that when I was a lad, 'all' nurses were women and looked like Barbara Windsor or Shirley Eaton.

And then it dawned on me that this friend was the same friend who claimed that his Jimi Hendrix poster had fallen down on to the floor of his room at the precise moment on the exact anniversary to the minute of great guitarist's death a few years earlier and I came to the conclusion that, sadly – oh so very sadly – my friend had allowed his fantasies to get the better of him ... and me.

So I was going to dismiss the question altogether as an urban myth but then my conscience got the better of me and, with no little trepidation, I sent an email to the Royal College of Nursing, the nurses' professional body.

I got a call back from a very nice press officer named Colin. 'Do you want the short answer?' he asked.

My ears pricked up. Yes please.

'No.'

Is that it?

'Well, could you please add that nurses are highly professional practitioners and this is certainly something that is not within their remit.'

Curses!

Hello,

I wonder if you can help me.

My name's Mitchell Symons and I'm an author (check me out on www.amazon.co.uk). I'm currently writing a light-hearted book answering all sorts of questions – many supplied by readers of previous books.

One of these is this: Is it true that nurses will 'relieve' a patient who can't oblige himself?

This might seem frivolous or even impertinent – most of the questions are – but that doesn't mean that I don't do my utmost to answer them as authoritatively as possible. Hence this email to you.

My telephone number is ...

Very best wishes,
Mitchell Symons

Can eunuchs have sex?

Fascinating question; prosaic answer. Some and some. Though there aren't too many around these days – harems not being as common as they once were – eunuchs have always fallen into two types: those without balls who could still have sex (even if their chat-up lines might be a bit shrill) and those without any tackle at all who, er, couldn't.

And that's that.

Why are prostitutes called hookers?

This is really simple. As everyone knows, prostitutes are called hookers because, during the American Civil War, General Hooker wouldn't allow prostitutes – or camp followers – to accompany his troops. Consequently, as an act of revenge, his men called such women 'hookers'.

Nice story. But it isn't true.

It has absolutely nothing to do with the general as the word 'hooker' was used to mean 'prostitute' *before* the Civil War.

Apparently, the origin of the word is that prostitutes used to trap or 'hook' their clients – hence 'hooker'.

Not as much fun as the general but much more accurate.

Are there any animals – apart from man – that have sex for recreation rather than procreation?

According to my zoologist chum Lucy, not many – at least, not many if you apply the strict definition to 'recreation' that there must be no chance of procreation and also that both males and females are willing participants.

'In fact,' says Lucy, 'the only two mammals that fit those criteria are dolphins and bonobos.'

Bonobos?

'They're apes.'

OK. How come other animals don't go in for sex on a recreational basis?

'Wrong question! You shouldn't be asking me why nearly all animals *don't* have sex recreationally but why humans *do*?'

Please explain.

'Recreational sex is a luxury in which few species can indulge. Think about it: other animals are far too busy gathering food to have purely recreational sex and, if they had the time, why would they waste their energy on something so non-productive?

'There's another factor too: when animals mate, they often have to fight other animals for the right to mate – females as well as males. Now while that's justifiable for them where reproduction is at stake, it wouldn't be worth it just for fun.'

But bonobos and dolphins know better, do they?

'They're more evolved and therefore more like us – though why bonobos and not other members of the ape family should go in for recreational sex, I can't tell you.'

... And following on from that, do any other animals masturbate, and are there any other animals – besides man – that are sometimes gay?

I wasn't letting Lucy go that easily!

Well?

'The answer is yes and no.'

I don't want that sort of answer!

'Tough, because it's the only answer you're going to get! Obviously, with masturbation – as opposed to recreational sex – there isn't the same risk of being attacked by a rival animal. However, the other factors I mentioned – like a disinclination to waste time, energy or, indeed, useful sperm – would inhibit such behaviour.'

What about our old dog Blue, a daft Golden Retriever that used to hump legs, clothes, furniture – anything? He didn't stop wanking: put me off cannelloni for years.

'Domestic pets – especially male dogs – *are* different. There's no doubt about that and a male dog will behave much the same as his male owner ...'

Steady on there, Lucy.

'It's also true that monkeys will indulge in group masturbation. I think what we see emerging from all this is that where animals have the time and the energy, they'll also have the inclination.'

So what about the other part of the question: do other species also have homosexual animals?

'Well, I mentioned the monkeys and the group masturbation, and there have been quite a few examples of gay monkeys and claims made for all sorts of other animals – even including penguins. I think we have to take many of these cases with a pinch of salt as there is a great tendency to anthropomorphize animal behaviour: to make it tie in with our own.'

Would that explain why so many of these 'gay couples' are found in zoos in American cities with a high gay population?

'I think it would. What we call homosexual behaviour might just be the result of distress or simply play or grooming. It's interesting to note what happens when female monkeys are introduced into a so-called male partnership.'

What happens?

'The monkeys revert to heterosexual type.'

Vice is nice but incest is best. Discuss.

Don't be silly. This is an old gag (if it can be so distinguished) that masks a truly evil act.

Mind you, while we're on the subject of gags, wasn't it once said that you should try everything once – except incest and morris dancing?

I've never had any inclination to do either. But then you should see me dancing – and, indeed, my sisters and mother (sorry, girls!).

This was obviously a deeply unpleasant topic to research – and one I put off for some time. It was also an area where the internet – usually so useful – was not a good idea because, beyond straight definitions 'sexual intercourse between persons too closely related to marry', so much of the material on the subject is pornographic and therefore totally unhelpful.

So I consulted my vast library of sexual books – accumulated over a number of years for instances just like this – and talked with a doctor, a psychiatrist and a social anthropologist.

There are obviously different forms of incest – father–daughter is probably the most prevalent but brother–sister is also relatively common.

Two things we can say for sure: it has very little to do with sexual appetite and everything to do with control, identity and individual family dynamics – particularly when that family is dysfunctional.

The other thing to know is that it cuts across class. This surprised me, because I had always understood there to be two types – stereotypes – of incest. The first is the working man who comes home from the pub drunk and demands sex from his wife, who refuses, and so he turns to his daughter instead. The other stereotype I was aware of harks back to the large working-class families of the 1930s where brothers and sisters found themselves in positions of enforced intimacy.

True as both of those (types of) stories might be, they are not the whole picture. The upper-class father is no less likely to abuse his daughter than his working-class counterpart – though maybe he doesn't have to get drunk first. Similarly, brother–sister or mother–son liaisons can occur in any type of family – particularly (in the case of brothers and sisters) in broken families.

The fact that incest is relatively rare in (what we might term) civilized societies is because – for all sorts of important evolutionary reasons – a disinclination to have sex with close relatives is hardwired into our DNA. It is even said that brothers and sisters are programmed to be sexually turned off each other's pheromones.

Nevertheless, it does happen.

So where does it all start?

Right at the beginning.

The Bible is full of incest. If you're going to be literal about it, if Adam and Eve had three sons, how did the human race continue without at least one of the lads having sex with his mum?

But even apart from that, Abraham married his half-sister, while his brother married his own niece. Meanwhile, Lot was seduced by his daughter, who plied him with wine in order to 'preserve the seed'.

Moving swiftly forward through the years, we find Caligula raping one of his sisters.

Then there's Lord Byron who had an incestuous – and, indeed, adulterous – relationship with his half-sister.

Casanova fell in love with a teenage girl whom he later discovered was his daughter by an earlier conquest. He also once wrote, 'I have never been able to understand how a father could tenderly love his charming daughter without having slept with her at least once.'

There is also strong evidence that Victor Hugo had a sexual relationship with his daughter.

Adolf Hitler had an affair with his half-sister's daughter, who eventually killed herself.

After the comic actor Arthur Mullard died, his daughter revealed that he'd frequently forced himself upon her when she was younger.

Clara Bow's father was mentally sick and, mistaking his daughter for his wife, had sex with her when she was 16. Rita Hayworth was also the victim of her father.

All in all, I think even morris dancing is preferable.

Why have I never had a wet dream ...

(Not even as a teenager.)

Unless it has happened to you too, you can have no idea how bewildering it was as a teenager to hear the other lads going on about their wet dreams.

Oh I would snigger – I was a fine sniggerer – and make all the right noises in those discussions but I was just pretending.

While every other boy in the class was experiencing nocturnal emissions on a seemingly endless basis, I was waking up bone dry with spotlessly clean sheets.

Was there something wrong with me, I wondered?

It was only years later – in fact, about five minutes ago if I'm honest – that it occurred to me that other boys too might have been dissembling. Who knows – maybe we were all making it up?

I decided to go back to the master: Kinsey. According to his findings, 83 per cent of men had experienced wet dreams or nocturnal emissions – most frequently in their teens, with a decline by the time they reached their 30s. The figure for women and nocturnal orgasms was 37 per cent – which was higher than I'd have thought. Incidentally, 13.11 per cent of males (compared to 5 per cent of females) had their very first ejaculation in the form of a nocturnal emission (orgasm).

So it seems that most of them – in fact, 83 per cent of them – weren't making it up. I was just one of the 17 per cent.

Still, it proves I was right to assume that my teenage years were the most likely to produce a wet dream – which is some (but not much) consolation.

What is it with porn stars and their names?

I have actually met a porn star. She was an English woman named Linda who used her maiden name to make porn films and her married name for her painting (she was a seriously talented artist). Or it might have been the other way round – but you get my drift. I was sent to interview her by the editor of *Penthouse* magazine some 20 years ago. Can't think why I was chosen as I rarely did (or, indeed, do) interviews – I'm much too interested in my own views – and I've never been especially interested in porn films (as a former TV director, I'm far too aware of the technical exigencies to be able to suspend disbelief).

Still, there I was and there she was: attractive, intelligent and very frank. As I recall, our only disagreement arose when she claimed that porn films were no different from any other kind of film. She compared her films to westerns – asking me why I was so fascinated about her having sex in her films when I don't make any fuss about John Wayne shooting people in his films. In both instances, she averred, it was only acting.

I wasn't having any of it. 'Hang on, when John Wayne shoots someone, they get up at the end of the take; when you fuck someone, they stay fucked.'

She couldn't – or wouldn't – see my point and we agreed to disagree. I wrote my profile and she sent me a lovely letter thanking me for writing an insightful piece.

And now, for the life of me, I can't remember her surname. But I do know that it was something terribly ordinary – like Jones or Davies or something like that.

These days, porn stars – of both genders – have the most extraordinary names.

Try these – just as examples: Abbey Jewels, Nikki Charm, Chocolate

Delight, Holly Body, Koffee Kakes, Bubbalicious, Horny Henry, Lisa Lipps, Wendy Whoppers, Abundancy Jones, Brandi Wine, Juicy Fruit, Bunny Bleu, Big Daddy Porn, Gwendy Licious, Tiffany Towers, Hope Rising, Amber Angel, Johnny Rocket, Sharon Swallow, April Showers, Darling Desire, Blonde Ice, Ebony Ayes, Purple Passion, Long Dong Silver, Aphrodite Night, Crystal Sky, September Raines, Kayla Kleavage, Agent 69, Quentin Cream, Autumn Haze, Fantasy Kiss – and there are thousands more like that out there.

Indeed, there are even ways of 'working out' what your porn name would be (if you decided to pursue a career in that field – or, rather, that seedy apartment). Either use your middle name or your first pet as a first name and the (first) name of the street you grew up on as your surname. This means I would be Paul Green or (much better) Snowy Green.

Silly porn star names – and my apologies to any of the above who were actually thus christened – are the fun part of what many people consider to be a pretty tawdry (if lucrative) business.

If you doubt the tawdriness then consider the effect that video and digital equipment has had on the market. Now that anyone can participate in porn films, anyone does. This has led to the rise of what might be called Gonzo film-making and increased competition. In turn, these have led to much more sexual recklessness.

Put it this way, whereas my generation was more than satisfied with Sven and Hans saying to a couple of girls, 'You want to come back to our place and party?', followed by 20 minutes of straight sex and simple cum shots (also known as 'money shots'), people today obviously demand more.

Something like 'double anal penetration' may be legal and female porn stars (not necessarily the ones I've named above) might happily consent to being thus penetrated. However, the harm done to their bodies – even and including a retirement spent wearing colostomy bags

– renders the whole bloody thing beyond the pale as far as I'm concerned.

In other words, I regard it as perfectly proper for consenting adults to watch other consenting adults having pleasure but not to watch them inflicting – and receiving – pain.

For these are not westerns and when the shooting stops, the pain continues.

Even for those 'stars' who don't get physically messed up, the future isn't necessarily that rosy.

As you can imagine, I collected those porn stars names off the internet. I clicked on to one – not one I've listed – at random, only to discover that she's currently serving three to five years in a state penitentiary for burglary.

Glamorous it isn't.

Tiffany Towers
Wendy Whoppers
Long Dong Silver
Quentin Cream

... And why are the men in porn movies so ugly?
(When you figure there's no shortage of applicants.)

You know those old-fashioned porn films I referred to in the previous answer? The ones starring a pair of bearded Germans/Dutchmen and a pair of obliging blonde girls?

Well, tell me that those blokes weren't ugly, eh? And fat. And lousy – truly lousy – actors who couldn't even deliver their sole line – 'You want to come back to our place and party?' – with anything approaching verisimilitude.

Even their coital grunting and groaning – 'You're soooo good' – sounded about as convincing as a politician's promise.

Watching these films on a flickering screen or, later, on a primitive video recorder, my friends and I would wonder at the casting: 'We're better-looking than them,' we would shout. 'We could be doing that!'

Maybe these blokes' ugliness was the USP (unique selling point) for such films: if girls would put out to/for them, then just think what they would do for us!

Later, we would rationalize that perhaps the men got their parts (so to speak) because they could perform while others were watching, that they could keep it up again and again and that they had improbable stocks of semen.

Well, either that or they were friends of the director.

Viagra has changed all that.

Now, any man can stay erect for as long as, er, the part requires. All day every day.

Oooooh Ja baby!

Viagra will keep blood flowing to the parts that other remedies can't reach.

No need for the 'fluffers', who used to have to get or keep the actors aroused; no more cries of 'Got wood!' as an actor finally gained/regained his erection.

The only problem is that Viagra doesn't help a man produce any more cum than he would otherwise have but that's where the miracle of film-making comes in: cum shots can be cut in – albeit shot from different angles – and then reused (*ad nauseam*).

Viagra means that the porn industry no longer has to rely on ugly men who can keep it up but can instead select men on the basis of their looks and the size of their penises.

Why, they could even choose men on the basis of their acting ability (although I wouldn't bet on it).

There are still, I am told, 'ordinary Joes' employed in skinflicks but, nowadays, they're not ugly sods and they don't have to be called Sven or Hans.

'Got wood!'

Das is hot.. yeah!

Is it true that women's hairy nipples get hairier if women remove the hairs?

Oh God, is there *anything* more disgusting than hairy nipples?

There you are, back at some girl's place. You start snogging and groping and – saints be praised! – she responds (or, at the very least, lets you continue). One thing leads to another and – yes! – there's that fantastic moment when you realize that you're going to have sex with her.

Feverishly, you undress each other while simultaneously taking care not to miss a single erogenous zone when … you discover that she has hairy nipples.

Aaaargh!!!

As far as I'm concerned, hair is a no-no on women – apart from on heads (the more the better) and 'down there' (a well-trimmed triangle). But then, when it comes to women, I'm with Germaine Greer, 'However much body hair a woman has, it is too much' (although I suspect that she wasn't coming at the subject from *quite* the same angle).

When you broach this subject with women, one of their standard responses is to say, 'Ah yes, but if you start removing hairs, they only come back even stronger!'

To which you groan and say (*sotto voce*), 'Small price …' but you've lost and the conversation has to move on.

So is it true?

According to tricologist Frank Cunningham, it's not. 'The plain answer is no. Cutting or shaving hair from nipples or the upper lip does not increase growth potential. In both cases, though, I would recommend electrolysis to stop the hairs growing permanently.'

I accept that electrolysis is not fun. A fine needle is placed down the hair shaft into the hair follicle and then a mild electric current is passed through to kill the follicle. Each hair has to be killed individually and because only a limited number of hairs can be killed during any one session, it could take many sessions to cure the problem.

However, if it's going to remove hair from the nipples or the upper lip permanently, then surely it's got to be worth it?

Unless you're the sort of woman who wants to be with the sort of man (or woman) who likes that kind of thing. In which case you're welcome to each other.

How do prostitutes who cater for men who want to dress up as babies keep a straight face?

This was tossed into the book as a bit of light relief – an opportunity for me to have a giggle with a prostitute who specializes in this sort of thing.

So I phoned up my old friend Mistress Mia who, according to her listing, offers services such as smoking fetishes, boot worship and verbal humiliation, and I kicked off the conversation by asking her why I would go to her for verbal humiliation when I can get that at home.

Tee hee: so far, so lighthearted.

However, when I moved on to the specific question about men dressing up as babies, she didn't seem to want to join in.

Misinterpreting her reluctance as sympathy for men who like to do that sort of thing, I remarked that it seemed harmless enough.

'No,' she said, 'you don't understand. I don't do it because you get men who want to fill their nappies and I don't do hardsports.'

And then the penny dropped. I had assumed that when men dressed up as babies, it was all a bit of a joke – because I found it funny. It was only when I found myself talking to someone who's involved in it all that I realized just how serious the whole thing is – for all parties.

Because I consulted a prostitute instead of a punter on this question, my empathy (and sympathy) is with the former and I can see – all too clearly – how they would have absolutely no difficulty in keeping a straight face. Perhaps the question should have been: How Do They Keep The Disgust Off Their Face?

And before anyone – yes, Rick, especially you – chides me for being buttoned-up or judgemental, can I say that although I recognize that coprophilia exists and there's nothing wrong with consenting adults indulging in it, I am also entitled to exercise my rights, which include the right to find certain practices disgusting.

Is there such a thing as sex after marriage?

Oh God, I know, I'm just asking, but it's depressing me even to think about it. Put it this way, after talking to my closest ten (male) friends and canvassing them on when they last 'did' it and how often they 'do', it isn't very encouraging.

Now, at this point, I should probably 'fess up to the frequency of my own sex life. However, my wife – and it does take two, you know – is understandably reluctant to share the secrets of our intimacy with you (or, indeed, anyone else).

So all I will say is that my experience is no different from my friends' – although my sad male ego obliges me to say that I'm getting it more than most of them.

Which, alas, isn't saying much.

Look, the latest (2005) studies prove what any of us could have told the researchers in the first place: passion doesn't last forever.

According to Dr Enzo Emanuele, the man who led the study at the University of Pavia, the chemical in our brains that characterizes intoxicating passion wears off after a year. Dr Emanuele's researchers studied a group of men and women aged 18–31: some were single, some had recently fallen in love and some were in long-term relationships.

The new lovers had high levels of the protein known as Nerve Growth Factor (yup, this is the one that causes the sweaty palms, the euphoria and the palpitations). The couples who had been together for over a year had the same low levels of NGF as the single people.

Dr Emanuele's report concluded: 'Given the complexity of the sentiment of romantic love and its capacity to exhilarate, arouse, disturb and influence so profoundly our behaviour, further investigations on the neurochemistry and neuroendocrinology of this unique emotional state are warranted.'

Of course.

But where does this leave us – and, by us, I mean *us*. I guess it proves that while there can be sex after marriage, that sex is likely to be more compassionate than passionate, reassuring more than all-consuming.

And here's the rub: these are the – in all senses of the word – 'best' marriages. The relationships I know of where they have the most (shall we say) vigorous sex are usually the most fraught: the ones living on the edge.

Nope, as a man who's old enough to remember when sex *before* marriage was an issue, I'll gladly settle for the deep comfort of the double bed over the hurly burly of the back seat of the car.

And, having paraphrased Mrs Patrick Campbell, let me now commit the greater literary crime of adapting Philip Larkin.

Sexual intercourse ended

In nineteen eighty-three

(Which was rather early for me)

Between the end of *The Romans In Britain* ban

And The Beastie Boys' first CD

Is there such a condition as nymphomania or is it merely a cherished male fantasy?

Maybe the word 'or' shouldn't have been included in the question – for whether or not the condition exists, it will always be a cherished male fantasy.

Why? Because the idea of a woman who's always up for it is mightily appealing … until, that is, you actually meet such a woman and discover the hard (or soft) way that you can never make her happy.

I've never (knowingly) met any nymphomaniacs but my friend Rick the satyr (and they don't come much more satyrical than Rick) has and he tells me that it was 'abso-fucking-lutely terrifying. I mean, I thought I had an appetite but she was insatiable!'

The dictionary definition of nymphomania is 'a disorder in which a woman exhibits extreme or obsessive desire for sexual stimulation or gratification', but since the condition is a non-medical one, an equally useful definition might be 'any woman who wants more sex than the man/men she's hooked up with'.

The key word – and the one that terrifies even satyrs – is 'obsessive'.

I mean, meaningless, dispassionate sex doesn't bother most men – in fact, if we're honest, we spend our lives searching for just such a thing – but if it comes courtesy of a monomaniacal, bunny-boiling compulsive, then count us out.

The first full-length study of nympho-mania, *Nymphomania, or a Dissertation Concerning the Furor Uterinus,* was written by an 18th-century French doctor named M. D. T. De Bienville.

He was of the opinion that the condition was caused or exacerbated by 'dwelling on impure thoughts', eating rich food (especially chocolate), reading novels and, of course, performing 'secret pollutions' (i.e. playing with themselves).

Throughout the 19th century, women 'suffering' from the condition of nymphomania were treated much in the same way as boys caught masturbating (see page 30: Why Did People Think That Masturbation Made You Blind?).

Perhaps we should leave the last word to Alfred Kinsey, whose definition of a nymphomaniac was 'someone who has more sex than you do'.

... And, while we're on the subject, what's the male equivalent of nymphomania?

I've already introduced the concept of the satyr – defined as 'a man with strong sexual desires'. Well, that's not at all dissimilar and, if you remove the genders, it might even be a matter of conjugation: *I* have a healthy appetite, *you* have strong sexual desires, *she's* a raving nymphomaniac.

One important difference between satyrs and nymphomaniacs is that the former are (supposedly) in control of their sexuality – but, then again, this distinction probably reflects society's suspicion of female sexuality.

Don Juanism – the desire by a man to have sex very frequently with many different partners – is another word for Satyriasis. It's named after the libidinous literary character Don Juan, who was immortalized by Byron in a poem and Mozart in an opera (*Don Giovanni*).

There is another term – again used mostly for men – and that's 'sex addict'. In recent years, several Hollywood stars – all men – have been named in the press as suffering from 'sex addiction'. Some of them are even said to have been treated in clinics.

Excuse me for not buying into this, but I don't think so. The truth is that the sort of person who becomes a star is often larger than life – with appetites to match. In Hollywood, everyone gets screwed and everyone gets laid and it doesn't depend on location. It was ever thus. Nowadays, however, the press doesn't turn a blind eye and so when male stars get caught *in flagrante*, they'd better have a good excuse for their wives or else, under Californian law, they're going to lose half of everything.

How much easier to cop a plea of 'sex addiction' and rest up for a few weeks in a clinic.

If a gay man marries a lesbian, who does the washing-up?

Incredibly, I happen to know a gay man who's married to a lesbian but, alas, I don't know him well enough to ask him the question. However, having observed the pair of them, I have no doubt that he does the washing-up – and the drying and the putting away too.

However, that's merely a reflection on them and their relationship. He's a talented, kind, easy-going sort of bloke, while she's a champion ball-breaker. I can see what she sees in him but God knows what he gets from her – unless there's a sub/dom thing going on of which I'm not aware.

The world of celebrities isn't of much help either. The gay Hollywood star Robert Taylor married the lesbian (or bisexual) Hollywood star Barbara Stanwyck, while the gay Paul O'Grady (aka Lily Savage) married a Portuguese lesbian named Teresa, but this was, by all accounts, a marriage of convenience and they subsequently divorced.

So where does that leave us?

In a rather unsatisfactory place.

Obviously, for the sake of the book – no less than for my *amour propre* – I want to know that gay men are more likely to be pussy-whipped than straight men. While at the same time, it would be pleasing to know that lesbians are tougher on men than straight women are.

Who knows, maybe some gay men and lesbians conform to such outdated stereotypes. But I'm gradually learning not to bet on it.

In real life, there's no reason to believe that gay men are any more helpful around the house than the rest of my gender and there's no reason to believe that lesbians are any more assertive than their heterosexual sisters.

This is one impertinent question that doesn't produce a pertinent answer.

Unless, that is, it just did.

What did women use before sanitary towels?

Yeah, right? And what do I know of women and periods (besides the fact that they're best avoided during them)? Precisely.

Fortunately, I happen to be married to someone who is not only a woman (no surprises there) but also a fine writer and researcher. So it's over to Penny Chorlton (her maiden name and the one she still uses professionally) for the answer:

Tampons of some description have been used for thousands of years – Hippocrates mentions them and the Egyptian peasants used either grass or papyrus for the purpose. Ancient Egyptian laundry lists mention cloth pads, belts and tampon-like items.

Until the 19th century, women feared blocking the flow (in case it caused intense bleeding). These must have been messy times.

Granny Rags, cloth pads made from old sheets, pillowcases or other surplus material, were folded and pinned into underwear and served the purpose for most women. When odour became an issue, the home-made pads could be boiled to clean them.

When they travelled, women either took their cloth pads home to wash or threw them in the fireplace. By the 1890s, there were special portable burners in England specifically for burning menstrual pads.

Then, around 1880, German doctors began proposing sanitary wear. But it was the Americans who patented the earliest menstrual protection devices in 1854. These consisted of belts with steel springs to hold a pad, which sound pretty cumbersome and uncomfortable. Mind you, considering the other corsetry women were wearing the idea wasn't outrageous. However, the products really didn't start gaining in popularity until the 1870s.

In 1890 American women could buy the first disposable pad, called 'Lister's Towel' (made by Johnson & Johnson). These had loops at either end and were worn with a belt – and nothing much changed for the next few decades. These pads leaked and were not particularly absorbent, which may help explain why periods became known as 'the curse' as they were just so difficult to manage. It's amazing it took everyone so long to come up with something better.

In World War One, nurses used large cotton pads to absorb blood from wounds of soldiers and would keep changing these as and when the need arose. Women soon started this practice to help deal with bleeding caused by menstruation.

The first commercial tampons were introduced in the 1920s but even up to the 1970s it was still considered more healthy to use sanitary pads to catch the flow outside the body rather than using something inside.

The first adhesive pads came in in the 1970s and then gradually the pads became thinner and yet more absorbent.

Natural sponges, animal hides, rags and old newspapers are still used in poorer parts of the world today.

What is the origin of the word 'camp' to describe effeminate behaviour?

Rather than approach the somewhat unapproachable Dr Karen Landy, I decided to do my own researches.

The Oxford English Dictionary (OED) gave 1909 as the first time that camp was used to mean 'ostentatious, exaggerated, affected, theatrical; effeminate or homosexual; pertaining to or characteristic of homosexuals'.

Later, by extension, it meant banality, vulgarity or artificiality when deliberately affected, especially with humorous overtones. However, you can still see the link, because, for all sorts of reasons, homosexuals would almost certainly have had a greater sensitivity to nuance.

Like so many words, it is better defined by example than it is by strict definition. So *The Producers* is camp, *The Rocky Horror Picture Show* is camp, *Desperate Housewives* is camp. *The Sound of Music* became camp, *Batman* was camp on an adult level – as were The Monkees. Dame Edna Everage is camp, Elvis Presley (by the time he was playing Vegas) was unintentionally camp and Liberace was extremely camp –

all the more so because there were so many straight women of a certain age who really did think that Liberace was 'waiting for the right woman'.

The word 'camp' is closely related to the word 'kitsch' but while all things kitsch are necessarily camp, not all things camp are kitsch, because kitsch refers only to art, literature or music whereas camp covers everything from gay carnival floats to pink plastic flamingos.

According to the OED, the use of the word camp in this context is 'etymologically obscure'. However, there might be etymological (you don't think I'm going to let go of a word like that in a hurry) roots in the French verbs *camper,* which has a subsidiary meaning of 'to pose', and *se camper,* which has a subsidiary meaning of 'to put oneself in a bold, provocative pose'.

These roots cross-fertilized with the use of the word camp as 16th-century English theatrical slang for a male actor dressed as a woman (which was, of course, the norm in those days) and/or through the French word for countryside, *campagne,* because French travelling actors often dressed as women in the countryside.

Clearly, the key elements are drag, irony, a conversational style featuring bitchy retorts and malicious gossip and, perhaps most important, the certainty that you were part of a small group that was finding something extremely funny in something otherwise totally straight.

And since straight is the key word in that definition, it isn't hard to see how camp became so linked with gays and gay behaviour.

Why do some people enjoy being spanked and/or tied up?

'Hit me, hit me,' said the masochist.

'No,' said the sadist.

It's an old 'un but a good 'un.

In fact, according to the self-confessed sadist I consulted, that's the wrong answer. 'Hit them, I should say – but not necessarily when and where they're expecting.'

How, I wondered, did he manage to persuade women (for my anonymous source is straight) to be his victims?

'It's not what you think. Ultimately, it's about pleasure – for both of us – not lasting injury. I take extraordinary pains. Think about that sentence: really think about it.'

And the women come back for more?

'Usually. Put it this way, I'm normally the one who calls it quits.'

But then he is, of course, a sadist.

Although sadomasochism – defined as 'the derivation of pleasure from the infliction of physical or mental pain either on others or on oneself' – is relatively rare in practice, Kinsey discovered that 22 per cent of men and 12 per cent of women reported having an erotic response to a sadomasochistic story.

However, in any event, there's a lot more to the world of BDSM (see page 109) than sadomasochism.

And we Brits, who are (perhaps unfairly) characterized – even by ourselves – as a nation of spankers and 'spankees', are not alone.

According to research, some 11 per cent of American men and 17 per cent of American women (go figure) have reportedly tried bondage, while between 5 and 10 per cent of American adults go in for 'S&M' (i.e. light discipline) on an occasional basis.

Meanwhile, as my sadist source confirms, you don't need to be a sadist to enjoy a little hanky-spanky.

So I asked him, why do people do it?

'On one level, it's just fun – and you shouldn't underestimate the importance of fun in sex, but then there are other, more intense elements to it. It's all about control and the yielding of control during moments of heightened arousal. It's simultaneously exciting and intimate.'

What's the difference between S&M and bondage?

'Not a lot at the light level. S&M is, of course, sadism and masochism, but usually it just involves a bit of smacking and discipline. It helps if you went to public school.'

Isn't that stereotype a little out of date? You'd have to be at least 50 to have been beaten at school, no?

'I guess so, but there are an awful lot of men who pay dominatrices to give them a good seeing-to.'

But why? I was beaten at school and absolutely hated it. I'd pay good money *not* to be beaten again.

'That's one reaction: the other is to ensure that when you are beaten again, you're in control. Then there are other men who pay to beat prostitutes, but there are very few girls who are prepared to experience anything more than very light pain.'

You sound disappointed.

'I'm a little more ambitious.'

In what way?

'In terms of threshold of pain.'

But surely that's torture?

'Not when she's begging you for more! Obviously, I have to make sure before – and during – that she's absolutely fine with it but, ultimately, it's a matter of trust.'

And bondage?

'Although it's often used in conjunction with discipline, it doesn't involve any pain *per se*. Usually, it just means people getting tied up or restrained with handcuffs – that kind of thing. You should try it.'

If you say so.

'You are soooo boring!'

'Hit me, hit me,' said the masochist.

'No,' said the sadist.

What happens to prostitutes after they retire?

Of all the questions in this book, this was the one I found the most fascinating ... and the most frustrating.

I phoned several (current) prostitutes and went on to three different internet forums but was met with a mixture of blankness and hostility.

The blankness was, I concluded, due to three specific reasons:

1. **I was undoubtedly a tosser who was winding them up or trying to wangle a free sex call.**

2. **Even if I wasn't a tosser, why should they talk to me – for free (after all, they are prostitutes)?**

3. **Prostitution wasn't the career they dreamed about when they were younger. Very few women become prostitutes because their lives are going well. Consequently, even if they wanted to help me, it's highly unlikely that they'd have any idea of a life beyond prostitution.**

One girl – in her mid-20s – told me that she was planning to be a waitress one day, when she'd made enough money from prostitution. Now, I know it's axiomatic that you shouldn't deride other people's dreams just because they're cheap, but it's not much of an ambition, is it? I mean, it's not Julia Roberts in *Pretty Woman*. Nor is it Catherine Deneuve in *Belle De Jour* or Shirley Maclaine in *Irma La Douce*.

The only film – or, at least, the only one of which I'm aware – that showed the grim reality of prostitution was Tony Garnett's 1980 film *Prostitute*.

Research shows that the (mean) average working life of a prostitute is five years. Since this figure includes women who are (what one might call) semi-professionals – students, housewives etc. – whose careers are likely to be short-lived, this suggests that there are some women who spend decades working in what is euphemistically called the oldest profession, servicing, according to the same research, an average of 868 men per year. However, if you take out the part-timers, this would mean that there are some women 'seeing' thousands of men every year.

No wonder they don't want to talk to men phoning up claiming to be writers.

Obviously, the most common – common in the sense of usual – thing that retired prostitutes do is get married. Indeed, there used to be a saying that prostitutes make good wives, supposedly on the basis that 'practice makes perfect'.

I'd have thought that the contrary would be true: it must be very hard for them not to have a vestigial contempt for men in general which would hardly be conducive to a happy marriage.

This would hold true even in those cases – the majority – where the men were unaware of their wives' previous lives. Sometimes, however, they find out the hard way. In my researches, I came across the case of a man who married a woman who slept with men – for money – on their honeymoon. It turned out she was a hooker and couldn't break the habit. This might be an urban myth but I saw enough variations on the theme to be persuaded that there was some truth to it.

Meanwhile, here are some former prostitutes – well, they turned at least one trick – we know what happened to after they retired:

Nell Gwynne

Billie Holiday

Mata Hari

Eva Peron

Janis Joplin (in her teens, she tried – without much success – to sell herself for $5 a time. Later, when she was stranded away from home, she 'turned two tricks' to raise the money to get home)

Marilyn Monroe (as a (very) struggling actress in Hollywood, Marilyn would provide 'in-car sex' in exchange for restaurant meals)

Carole Landis

Jeanette MacDonald (worked as an 'escort' in New York before becoming famous)

Andrea Dworkin (the late feminist worked as a prostitute in the Netherlands in the early 1970s when she was extremely broke and the punters were clearly – forgive my lack of gallantry – even more desperate than she was)

Lupe Velez

Lotte Lenya (was a child prostitute)

What's so erotic about autoerotic asphyxiation?

In Beckett's *Waiting for Godot*, Estragon says to Vladimir, 'What about hanging ourselves?' to which Vladimir replies, 'Hmm, it'd give us an erection.' Estragon concludes by saying, 'Let's hang ourselves immediately!'

The first time many people – certainly in Britain – ever heard of this extraordinary practice was when the Conservative MP Stephen Milligan was discovered dead when the asphyxiation turned out to be more successful than the autoeroticism.

There were rumours too about the deaths of Jerzy Kosinski and Michael Hutchence.

In any event, it's clearly an awful way to check out – if only because it's so incredibly humiliating when it all goes wrong.

And that's the point, of course: we only tend to hear about autoerotic asphyxiation – or 'scarfing' as it's also known – in the breach. In other words, when something goes wrong.

So what precisely is it? I asked my friend Rick.

'It's self-strangulation – usually with a ligature or tourniquet to restrict blood flow – while masturbating. Some people – like Stephen Milligan – combine it with self-bondage. And that's just plain crazy.'

Had he himself, I wondered, tried it?

'No! Do I look like a complete arse? Hey, don't answer that question.'

So why do other men do it? And does it differ from the thrill you might get from dicing with death in any other way? In other words, is it just a case of (*pace* The Eagles) taking it to the limit?

'There's a lot of that to it, clearly. And I think that the process of restricting blood to the brain is in itself meant to heighten sexual pleasure. Me, I prefer a little bit of toot on the tip of …'

'All right, let's not go there.'

So why do people do it?

'Search me. It's mostly adolescent boys – or men who haven't quite grown up. It's terribly dangerous though. Loads of people die every year from it.'

How?

'The asphyxia bit. They lose control of their own consciousness and kill themselves unintentionally.'

So it's suicide?

'No, I don't think so. No more than any other extremely dangerous practice – like base jumping – is suicidal. It's about risk. Some of the men who do it rig up devices to wake themselves up in case they forget to breathe.'

Didn't Stephen Milligan use an orange or something?

'That's right but, alas, it didn't work ...'

What a way to go!

'Yes, it reminds me of that Bill Hicks routine where he says that, in the event of his unexpected death, he's instructed a friend to go round to his place and clear out all the porn – so that his mother doesn't see it.'

After talking with Rick, I did some research and discovered that autoerotic asphyxia (or AEA as it's known) claims the lives of between 250 and 1,000 young American men every year.

The reason why that figure is so vague is because parents of victims are understandably keen to have a different cause of death – anything, damn it – on the death certificate.

Interestingly – and even more tragically – the victims are usually well-adjusted, non-depressed, high achievers. There is also a tendency towards transvestism and other forms of dressing up/role play.

Girls too try AEA but much more rarely and because when they're found dead they tend to be naked with just the ligature around their necks, parents (understandably) assume suicide rather than sexual misadventure.

In 1981, FBI researchers Hazelwood, Blanchard and Burgess identified six defining characteristics of AEA typical death scenes for use by police investigators:

1   **Evidence of asphyxia produced by strangulation either by ligature or hanging, in which the position of the body or presence of protective means, such as padding about the neck, indicate that the death was not obviously intended.**

2   **Evidence of a physical mechanism for obtaining or enhancing sexual arousal and dependent on either a self-rescue mechanism or the victim's judgement to discontinue its effects.**

3   **Evidence of solo sexual activity.**

4   **Evidence of sexual fantasy aids, props or pornography.**

5   **Evidence of prior dangerous autoerotic practice.**

6   **No apparent suicide intent.**

How does a gigolo get a hard-on?

There are many gigolos out there – only they don't call themselves that. 'Male escort' is the usual euphemism – although many chaps advertise themselves as 'male masseurs'. According to Jake, the gigolo I ended up consulting, the difference between an escort and a masseur is that the former 'usually goes out for dinner with a lady before they have sex'.

So it's a bit more upmarket?

'Usually but not always: I've done both and I'd say the difference is that the ladies like it a bit – how can I put it? – raunchier when you go round to their place, which is usually a hotel room.'

At this point, I should introduce Jake. He's in his mid-30s and is a convivial chap. I wouldn't say he's handsome (as such) but the overall effect is a good one. He's clean and tidy and – as he points out to me – doesn't bite his nails. 'Unlike you – my God, you bite your nails so badly!'

On the contrary, I reply, I bite my nails extremely well. However, I think the subtlety is lost on him.

But it's certainly true that he's well turned out, in a dark jacket, pinstriped shirt, tie and chinos. 'I have to be, in my job. Even if I'm not working, I never know when I might get a call.'

Do you have regulars?

'Oh absolutely! There are five women I see regularly – perhaps twice a month.'

And do you always have sex with them?

'Usually, though there's one client who tends to use me to accompany her to business events – she's in the media or something and she has to go to lots of dinners.'

How does she describe you to people?

He thinks about it for a second. 'She doesn't really. I'm just Jake. I suppose she lets them think that I'm her boyfriend.'

What do you say if anyone asks you what you do for a living?

'I'd just say I was in business – which I suppose, in a way, I am. Funny thing is, people very rarely ask me.'

Too busy talking about their own careers?

He smiled in a noncommittal sort of way.

What about other clients?

'Yes, I have sex with them.'

And … ?

'It's fine.'

OK. Does it, er, work every time?

'For them? You bet! I know how to treat a lady like a lady.'

Suddenly, I was given an insight into how he can do what he does: you have to possess absolutely no sense of irony – and clearly the sort of man who can say, 'I know how to treat a lady like a lady' without blushing is an irony-free zone.

Do you use Viagra?

For the first time in our conversation, he looked annoyed. 'No, I don't. I don't have to.'

I'm sorry …

'No it's not your fault but people always assume …'

Well, it must be good to know that you could.

'I suppose so but who wants to walk around with an erection all evening?'

I see.

'I don't need it.'

What, never?

'No.'

Really?

He smiled and pointed down at his tool (the operative word): 'It's got a mind of its own. Also, I really do like my clients. I couldn't do my job properly if I didn't. It's not just about the sex, you see.'

Is a good wank better than a lousy blow job?

I had a lot of fun running this one past the lads, I can tell you.

Nearly all of them started off by saying that any blow job was better than a wank, but as soon as I invited them to be serious about it, they all concluded that a good wank was indeed better than a lousy blow job.

In fact, one or two went so far as to say that a good wank is better than a *good* blow job.

The arguments cited in favour of 'a good wank' included:

'You don't have to cuddle yourself afterwards.'

'You don't have to say thank you afterwards.'

'It's quicker.'

'You're not obliged to reciprocate.'

One friend said, 'Depends who's doing the blow job,' which is fair enough.

Another – how can I put this? – more intellectually challenged friend said, 'Depends who's doing the wank,' which is of course idiotic.

All in all, we can draw two conclusions from this scientific study. The first is that a good wank is better than a bad – or even an indifferent – blow job. The second is that my friends are a bunch of onanistic, misogynistic Neanderthals.

Well, why else would they be mates with me?

'You don't have to cuddle yourself afterwards'

What is uncircumcision?

Uncircumcision – or epispasm – is the process of restoring a foreskin. It is done for various reasons: cultural, sexual, psychological.

As most people know, Jewish male babies are circumcised soon after birth and so a circumcised penis has often served as a means of identification for those people hunting Jews – especially in societies like Nazi Germany, where non-Jews were rarely circumcised (and then only for medical reasons).

As a result of the Nazi persecution, many Jews in Occupied Europe resorted to extraordinary means to restore their foreskins so that, ultimately, they would pass scrutiny.

Some men were lucky enough to have (albeit rudimentary) surgery that involved skin grafts. Other men used tape to stretch what was left of their foreskins. Unfortunately for them, this process takes years before it produces any real results. Consequently, ever-desperate men were forced to adopt all kinds of subterfuge: the teenage Roman Polanski, for instance, fashioned a dummy foreskin out of candle wax.

Since the war, there have been other reasons for the practice of foreskin restoration. In the US especially, where circumcision was incredibly popular (though not necessarily with the boys who were having their foreskins sliced off) throughout the 1950s and 1960s, there have been many men who have subsequently seen themselves as victims of medical fashion.

Such men turn to a variety of remedies in their drive to return to what they see as a 'whole state'.

Nowadays, there are many surgical and non-surgical means by which foreskins can be effectively replaced.

The current medical thinking is that circumcision is harmless but unnecessary. According to a (Jewish) urologist I consulted, 'If people want to circumcise their baby sons for religious or cultural reasons then that's fine, but otherwise there's no reason to.'

Aren't circumcised penises cleaner?

'Yes, but that's no argument for cutting off foreskins – any more than you'd cut off fingers because they can get dirty. Boys just have to be taught to wash themselves thoroughly. Same's true for men like us: just because we haven't got a prepuce ...'

A what?

'It's the posh word for foreskin. Anyway, just because we haven't got one between us doesn't mean we don't have to keep ourselves clean.'

But don't some boys have to be circumcised when they're older because their foreskins are too tight?

'Yes – and your point is?'

Well, isn't it better to circumcise them when they're babies because it would be less painful?

'By that logic, you'd also whip out their appendix and their tonsils – oh and their spleens and their gall bladders, just in case.'

So if in doubt, best not to circumcise?

'I'd say so – unless there's a religious imperative and, even then, I'd have it done in a hospital.'

What about female circumcision?

'Don't go there.'

Really?

'Yes, there is absolutely no advantage to it and the only reason why it's practised is to subdue women.'

Clearly you feel strongly about it.

'Yes I do – and so should everyone.'

Does penis size vary with ethnicity?

If I'm honest, this is really just a polite way of asking, 'Are black men better endowed?'

When I told friends that I was doing this book, I asked them for possible questions – and this was one that raised its ugly head (so to speak) more than once.

There's surprisingly little data on the subject and you'd better believe that I wasn't about to start looking on the internet (there are some things I'm not prepared to do – even in the name of research).

So I contacted the world's greatest authority – the Kinsey Institute – to ask this question and they wrote back to say: 'As for penis size, yes, there are ethnic variations, as there are for most body parts.'

Which sounds fair enough.

The original 1948 Kinsey Report found that the average white man's penis was 4 inches (non-erect) and 6.2 inches (erect), while the average black man's penis was 4.3 inches (non-erect) and 6.3 inches (erect). Not much of a difference – especially when erect – and it should be pointed out that Kinsey interviewed many more white men than black men.

So why do so many white people automatically assume that black men are better endowed? I decided to ask social anthropologist Dr Lorraine Mackintosh.

'Well,' she said, 'from what you tell me, they're not, so now we have to try to find out the reason for what is clearly a prejudice.'

A reverse prejudice, surely?

'A prejudice nonetheless. My guess is that it will have started when Africa was first explored by white people. They would have been fully clothed but the natives wouldn't have been and so they would have noticed their penises and, no doubt, remembered the bigger ones.

'Then we move to the United States during the days of slavery. Male slaves were treated as objects or animals and were often made to impregnate female slaves to produce new generations of slaves. So having been cast as sexual creatures – is it any wonder that the stereotype stuck?'

So clearly it's not a good thing.

'No, it isn't. Look, you're Jewish, right? Now although to tell someone that they're good with money is a compliment, if I said, "Hey, Mitch, you Jews are good with money" or made some other allusion to it, I don't think you'd be grateful.'

Well, I would, because I'm not particularly good with money.

'You know what I mean. I would be doing it to reinforce a stereotype that is, in turn, part of a whole series of stereotypes that were once used to victimize Jews.'

Just as being well endowed is part and parcel of the whole racism shtick.

All right, I accept that.

Is it morally worse for a man to rape a nun than a prostitute?

Having discussed this question on more than a few occasions, I've come to the conclusion that it is.

Although feminists, who tend to take an absolute line on this issue, hold that the rape of any or all women is equally repugnant, I think there is a difference.

First of all, I am not seeking to absolve the man who rapes a prostitute: he deserves to face the full weight of the law. However, there is, I believe, a different *quality* to the rape of a nun than there is to the rape of a prostitute.

Assuming, purely for the sake of argument, that in both cases the physical damage is equal – a rape committed with the threat of violence but without (as is so common in such cases) any additional injuries – one is left with the psychological damage done to the victim.

Without riding roughshod over the feelings of the prostitute, I would argue that, although she didn't consent to having sex with her assailant, the act of sex is not one that is foreign or (presumably) especially abhorrent to her.

For the nun, however, who has taken vows of chastity and celibacy, it might very well be much more harrowing.

By the same argument, it would be less traumatic for a millionaire to have £20 stolen than it would be for a pauper.

However, even as I write this, I am aware that my conclusions are, ultimately, based on instinct. True, I am a wise, intelligent man who wrote an award-winning opinion column for a national newspaper, but the only thing that separates me from the saloon bar pundit is that I have a platform for my views.

It's time to bring in an expert.

Nicholas Fearn is just the fellow. He's not only a brilliant philosopher – and the author of *Philosophy: The Latest Answers To The Oldest Questions* (thoroughly recommended) – he's also a thoroughly wise owl.

So, Nick, is it morally worse for a man to rape a nun than a prostitute?

I think it is. Stealing a car isn't made any more excusable just because the car happened to be up for sale at the time. On the other hand, it would be worse to steal one that you knew held sentimental value for its owner. So yes, raping a nun would be worse.

It reminds me of a different question I've been working on that you could phrase like this: does a rapist commit a less despicable act if he is incredibly handsome and charming than if he is ugly, weighs 17-stone and smells? Possibly, and it would be naive to think that this is not a factor in whether date-rates get reported. The male model has still done a terrible deed, but there is certainly some difference here. Whether we like it or not, the moral character of our actions depends to an extent on who and what we are. Everyone who works in an office knows this, as it is the difference between sexual harassment and flirting. If a homeless person steals a loaf of bread, his action is clearly different to that of a millionaire who steals it for the thrill. We are used to the debate being about whether the consequences of an action are what make it right or wrong, or whether the immorality is intrinsic to the act regardless of its repercussions. But the agent himself has been forgotten in all this, and for understandable reasons – for it would lead us to deny the principle of equality before the law and accept something that looks a lot like hypocrisy. Namely, that certain behaviour is indeed acceptable (or slightly less horrendous) for some and not others.

We are getting to a stage in this country where a lot of people would like freedoms to be selective and laws to be 'tailored'. For example, they would like the middle classes to be allowed to take drugs without the chief of police threatening to come and arrest them, but that doesn't mean they want a free-for-all. To deny the same rights to people on rough estates (those most likely to be harmed by drugs), or to those who have shown that they cannot handle the drugs' effects without harming others, is libertarian good sense rather than double standards. The law remains a one-size-fits-all institution in a day when there is no such thing as standard behaviour. But it's changing. What are ASBOs but selective laws prohibiting behaviour that is often normally allowed – such as going within 100 metres of the Lakeside shopping centre? One day they may be the rule and not the exception, though admittedly there will probably never be any tailoring when it comes to rapists.

That's the trouble with this question, as with so many others in this book – you ask one question and it raises a whole lot more.

Where do nudists keep their hankies?

It's a thought, isn't it?

After all, presumably nudists, or naturists as they call themselves, have to blow their noses from time to time – just like the rest of us.

So I wrote to Andrew Welch, the commercial manager for the Central Council for British Naturism, and received the following reply:

Bathing costumes, as far as I am aware, do not have pockets, so, on a beach, where does *anyone* keep their hanky?

Naturism is a healthy pursuit, naturists being attracted to the outdoor life and benefiting from regular exposure to fresh air and sunshine – the latter little and often, rather than the usual British thing of roasting for a fortnight on a once-a-year holiday – and so the incidence of colds is reduced … and therefore a reduced need for handkerchiefs anyway.

Naturism, in the UK especially, is also practised indoors in the winter months, in indoor pools, saunas, steam rooms and so on. The nature of this kind of activity is associated with warm places, but obviously, other than when enjoying the various facilities – typically a two- or three-hour session once a fortnight or so – naturists will be dressed the majority of the time in the winter, when colds are more likely to strike.

Even in the summer, though, naturism is mostly practised when the weather and circumstances are appropriate, and even in the hottest places many people will be dressed much of the time – slipping on a T-shirt in the heat of the day, putting on a pair of shorts for a visit to the on-site shop, dressing to make the journey to the local naturist beach or tourist attractions, and dressing to eat in the on-site restaurant in the evenings when the sun has gone down. In fact, strange though it may sound, most naturist holiday resorts around the world insist on clothes being worn when dining in the evenings.

I think there is an assumption that naturists are always naked. I'm sure there are some that take the opportunity whenever and wherever they are, but the vast majority will only strip off when, as mentioned, the weather and circumstances are appropriate. They must also live within the norms of 21st-century Britain and that means being dressed outside the house, club, back garden, beach etc., and so for the majority of the time, there are plenty of places for a naturist to have a hanky.

Well, I think that answers the question.

POSTSCRIPT

So, what have I learned?

Firstly, that there's more to life than I thought.

From there, I think I've learned to accept more and judge less. However, when and where I do judge, I feel more entitled to do so more.

More specifically, I've learned the following:

- Not to underestimate the appeal of chocolate to women.

- The difference between a vow and a promise.

- Missionaries don't necessarily have sex in the missionary position.

- Women who have sex with other women are lesbians and *not* 'lesbian women'. Before writing this book I was guilty of that tautology.

- It's not a compliment to imply that black men have bigger penises than white men.

- The meaning of the word 'deracinate'.

- Naturists sometimes keep their clothes on.

ACKNOWLEDGEMENTS & BIBLIOGRAPHY

This book couldn't have been published without a lot of help. The key players were (in alphabetical order) Luigi Bonomi, Richard Carr, Penny Chorlton, Mari Roberts and last – but very much most – Doug Young.

In addition, I'd also like to thank the following people for their help, contributions and/or support: Gilly Adams, Jeremy Beadle, Marcus Berkmann, Paul Donnelley, Jonathan Fingerhut, Peter Freedman, Jenny Garrison, Ian Irvine, Brian Johnson, Sam Jones, Martin Lewis, William Mulcahy, Nicholas Ridge, Charlie Symons, Jack Symons, Louise Symons, David Thomas, Katrina Whone and Rob Woolley.

Apart from the internet and articles in newspapers and magazines, I relied heavily on advice and information from friends and colleagues whom I have credited above or as they appear in the text.

The books that follow – all of which I would have no hesitation in recommending to anyone interested in further reading – were extremely helpful, either directly or indirectly, and I would like to express my sincere thanks to the authors responsible.

The Secret Sex Lives of Famous People by Irving Wallace, Amy Wallace, David Wallechinsky and Sylvia Wallace (Cresset, 1993)

The Book of Sex Lists compiled by Albert B. Gerber (W.H. Allen & Co, 1981)

The Straight Dope by Cecil Adams (Chicago Review Press, 1984)

An Unhurried View of Erotica by Ralph Ginzburg (Martin Secker and Warburg, 1959)

Hollywood Lesbians by Boze Hadleigh (Barricade, 1994)

The Book Browser's Guide To Erotica by Roy Harley Lewis (David and Charles Ltd, 1981)

The Book of Erotic Failures by Peter Kinnell (Futura, 1984)

The Harlot By The Side of The Road, Forbidden Tales of The Bible by Jonathan Kirsch (Ballantine Books, 1997)

What Makes A Man G.I.B. (Good In Bed) by Wendy Leigh (Frederick Muller, 1980)

The American Sex Machines by Hoag Levins (Adams Media Corporation, 1996)

The Encyclopedia of Unusual Sex Practices by Brenda Love (Barricade, 1992)

Did She or Didn't She? by Mart Martin (Carol Publishing, 1996)

Hollywood Lovers edited by Sheridan McCoid (Orion Media, 1997)

Sex: An Illustrated Guide by Nicole Beland and Michael Carrera (Rodale International Ltd, 2005)

The Penguin Dictionary of Modern Humorous Quotations compiled by Fred Metcalf (Penguin, 1987)

The Juicy Parts by Jack Mingo (The Berkley Publishing Group, 1996)

Weird Sex compiled by Steve Moore (John Brown Publishing, 1995)

Men On Sex by John Nicholson and Fiona Thompson (Vermilion, 1992)

The Bumper Book of Sex by Ray Nunn (Wolfe Publishing, 1967)

Cultural Icons by James Park (Bloomsbury, 1991)

Doktor Bey's Handbook of Strange Sex by Derek Pell (Avon, 1978)

Working Girls: An Illustrated History of The Oldest Profession by Neil Phillip (Bloomsbury, 1991)

A Guide To America's Sex Laws by Richard A. Posner and Katherine B. Silbaugh (University of Chicago, 1996)

Sex Trivia: The Bedside Guide by Nicholas Reed (Take That Books/MaxiMedia, 1995)

Lesbian Lists by Dell Richards (Alyson, 1990)

The New Gay Book of Lists by Leigh W. Rutledge (Alyson, 1996)

The Kinsey Institute New Report On Sex by June M. Reinisch (Saint Martin's Press, 1998)

Romantic Love And Society by Jacqueline Sarsby (Penguin, 1983)

The Professionals by Iain Scarlet (Sidgwick and Jackson, 1972)

The Female Member by Kit Schwartz (Robson, 1988)

The Celebrity Sex Register by Shirley Sealy (Fireside, 1982)

The Simons Book of Sexual Records by G.L. Simons (W.H. Allen, 1975)

The Illustrated Book of Sexual Records by G.L. Simons (Virgin Books, 1982)

The Encyclopedia of Sexual Trivia by Dr Robin Smith (Robson, 1990)

The Book of Aphrodisiacs by Dr Raymond Stark (Stein and Day, 1981)

A Pictorial History of Love by Paul Tabori (Spring, 1966)

The Visual Dictionary of Sex by Dr Eric J. Trimmer (Pan, 1979)

Misalliance by Edward Abelson (Macdonald, 1989)

How Do They Do It? edited by Reinhold Aman (Maledicta, 1983)

Who's Had Who? by Simon Bell, Richard Curtis and Helen Fielding (Faber and Faber, 1987)

Entertainment Celebrity Register by Earl Blackwell (Visible Ink Press, 1992)

The Book of Royal Lists by Craig Brown and Lesley Cunliffe (Sphere Books, 1983)

The Naff Sex Guide by Dr Kit Bryson, Selina Fitzherbert and Jean-Luc Legris (Arrow, 1994)

Sex Lives of The US Presidents by Nigel Cawthorne (Prion, 1996)

The Guinness Book of Classic British Television by Paul Cornell, Martin Day and Keith Topping (Guinness, 1993)

The Dirty Bits by Lesley Cunliffe, Craig Brown and Jon Connell (Andre Deutsch, 1981)

Sexual Trivia by Sarah Curtis (Ward Lock, 1986)

The Unofficial Book of Political Lists by Iain Dale (Robson, 1997)

Sex: An Encyclopedia For The Bewildered by K.S. Daly (Aurum, 1995)

The English in Love: Passion Among The Elite by Anne De Courcy (Ebury Press, 1986)

TV Babylon by Paul Donnelley (Vista, 1997)

Sex Link by H.Y. Freedman (New English Library, 1978)

The International Dictionary of 20th Century Biography by Edward Vernoff and Rima Shore (New American Library, 1987)

Hotlips by Noelle Walsh (Ebury Press, 1985)

Looney Sex Laws by Robert Wayne Pelton (Walker, 1992)

Bluff Your Way In Sex by Tim Webb and Sarah Brewer (Ravette, 1987)

Dictionary of Erotic Literature by H.E. Wedeck (Peter Owen, 1962)

The Complete Book Of Sexual Trivia by Leslee Welch (Carol Publishing, 1992)

Sex Facts: A Handbook For The Carnally Curious by Leslee Welch (Carol Publishing, 1995)

Sex and Sexuality: A Thematic Dictionary Of Quotations by Alan Isaacs (Cassell, 1993)

PICTURE CREDITS